Trul

By Clay Damewood (Pentassuglia)

Clay and Cousin Martino: Greetings! *Saluti ed Auguri* **from Cisternino!**

ISBN: 1-59196-063-0

Printed in the US by Instantpublisher.com

Dedication:

I would like to acknowledge my Italian cousins, the Scarfile's and Simeone's, my family and supportive wife Eveline. I dedicate this cookbook in memory of my Grandfather, Angelo Antonio Pentassuglia who immigrated to the USA, a country he dearly loved, in the early 1900's in order to provide his family a better life.

Below: Nonno Angelo and Nonna, Maria Nicola Scarafile, with my Uncle Dan.

Table of Contents

iii

Meat-Based Sauces 63-103

Seafood-Based Sauces 106-127

INTRODUCTION

As an Italian-American I wrote *TRULLI ITALIAN* to offer unpretentious menus and methods to prepare authentic Italian pasta dishes in the home-made or *"alla casalinga"* style from the region of Apulia (*Puglia*) in Southern Italy. The *Trullo* house pictured on the cover can only be found in Apulia. These structures dot the exotic and beautiful countryside in the Valley of Itria and are national monuments. I wanted to bring you some of the recipes my relatives make there to this day. This is not a regional cookbook in the true sense of the word, although I wanted to expose the reader to the history and culture of the region of Apulia (*Puglia*). My main effort is to translate the ingredients found in Italy to the American table to the greatest extent possible. In my experience food always tastes differently in its native environment and is not easily imitated in foreign lands. For example, *mozzarella di bufala* or mozzarella cheese from Naples can only be found in the region of Compagnia where water-buffaloes are used to make this delicious, soft cheese. My recipes do not contain exotic ingredients but rather economical off-the-shelf ingredients and easy methods for preparing great tasting dishes, some traditional and some new, with preparation times for the most part of 30 minutes or less.

I also wanted to dispel many myths about the complexity of Italian cooking. I lived in Northern and Southern Italy for over seven years experimenting with friends, relatives, and in *trattorie* and restaurants discovering practical tips in preparing the best Italian dishes adapted to ingredients readily available to the average American. *"Arte Casalinga"* or home cooking in its purest form uses fresh ingredients whenever practicable, with simple, quick uncomplicated preparation directions. You don't need fancy utensils, a pasta maker, or tubs of fresh chicken broth in your refrigerator to execute great recipes. Italians subtly use spices, herbs, tomatoes, and other flavorings to make their sauces delicately accent the pasta it is served with. I will share with you common do's and don'ts of real "old country" Italian cooking which if adhered to can make a significant difference in the way your pasta dishes turn-out.

Many cookbooks include exciting recipes but for most of us it becomes an overwhelming task to gather up all the special ingredients needed for each recipe. Included in *Trulli Italian* is a comprehensive shopping list, which will allow you to go to your local supermarket and buy most all of the ingredients in one trip for the recipes contained within this cookbook. I also will list the minimum types of utensils needed in an Italian kitchen, which herbs and spices to stock, how to use them and the different types of cheeses used in Italy. From my *Pugliese* cousins I bid you *Auguri, Saluti* and

BUON APPETITO!

My cousin's Martino and Giovanni in front of my Grandfather's centuries old *Trullo* house called *Truddhi* in local dialect. *Trullo* means, "domed hall" in Greek. Generally, the architectural style of these national monuments are thought to have been transplanted from the Greek Byzantine Empire to Apulia in the 700's but existing Bronze age structures called *Specchie* indicate earlier origins.

Apulia: Terra Fortunata

Dante referred to Apulia (*Puglia* in Italian) as the fortunate land. Today Apulia (*Puglia*) is slowly being discovered by the rest of the world. Each year hordes of Northern European tourists are flocking to the region because of its dry, Mediterranean climate, hospitality of the locals, history, architecture, and cuisine. Apulia is known as the heel of the boot of Italy that divides the Adriatic and Ionian seas. My grandparents emigrated from the beautiful Valley of Itria to the United States in the early 1900's. The Valley of Itria runs north to south inland from Bari to Brindisi. It is a rocky plateau, which overlooks the coastline of the Adriatic Sea. My relatives live to this day in Cisternino, which is southwest of Bari and northwest of Brindisi. The town of Cisternino enjoys spectacular views of the Valley of Itria. The western-side is dotted with *Trulli* houses and from the eastern flank one can gaze upon the beautiful beaches and Adriatic Sea.

Cisternino or in Latin *Cisternum* for cistern or well has a complex history. Basilican Monks originally established a monastery in Cisternino. Today remnants of the Aragonese Spanish fortress walls that once surrounded the whole city can still be seen. The town is whitewashed and resplendent in the strong sunlight. Throughout the ages, different invaders realized the strategic importance of the small hill towns such as Cisternino as they lay claim to the town. The Romans fought the Tarantine Greeks on Monte Pagano, the Normans launched crusades to the holy land, the Aragonese Spanish and the Bourbon Angevin dynasties as well as the maritime empire of Venice occupied Cisternino at different times through out history as one empire's power eclipsed another's. The genetic influence can be seen in the inhabitants today, some of my cousins are dark and swarthy while others have light complexions and the red hair of the Norman French crusaders. From one

3

village to another the dialects become almost incomprehensible. *Cistranese* or the Cisternino dialect of my Grandparents is a mixture of Norman French, Italian and other languages. In one nearby town a form of ancient Greek is still spoken.

At the center of the exotic beauty of undulating hills is a countryside dotted with the fairy-tale like *Trulli* houses. Declared national monuments by the Italian government the exact origin of the cone shaped structures is unknown. The following picture is of my late cousin Martino behind my maternal Grandfather's *Trullo* house. Basically, *Trulli* are farm dwellings. Crops and courtyard animals are raised all around the plots of land passed down from one generation to another.

Cousin Martino Simeone and background view of my Grandfather's *Trullo* house. The walls are made of limestone, as are the roof shingles on the *Trulli* houses. The shingles are called *"chiancarelle"*. The amazing fact about all *Trulli* houses is that they are made of un-mortared limestone blocks. Master stonemasons cut each block to act as a keystone latching into the next block.

THE ITALIAN KITCHEN

UTENSILS

You don't really need an elaborate set of utensils in your Italian Kitchen. The following lists the bare essentials in preparation of everyday meals. When choosing cookware try if at all possible to buy the better quality brands of pots and knives for several good reasons: in long run you get a much better return on investment by not having to replace items every year or so, and you will also be able to cook and prepare food in a more consistent manner. Food will less likely stick to the pans and cook at a more consistent temperature with good cookware. High quality sharp, stainless steel knives are actually safer than dull, cheap knives and will prevent cutting accidents if used properly. Stainless steel knives will not need to be sharpened like their carbon steel counterparts.

- *10 quart or larger heavy copper bottomed or stainless steel pasta pot*, preferably with separate metal colander. Thin-bottomed pots will burn the pasta that settles to the bottom while boiling. Heavier gage large pots prevent burning and provide plenty of water with which to cook the starchiness out of the pasta; otherwise the pasta could end up with a starchy taste and be off-colored.

- A *3-Quart saucepan* for cooking sauces. Also used to transfer the cooked pasta to the saucepan ingredients so that the flavor of the sauce is imparted into the pasta. This is a critical utensil! An over-sized sauté pan will work as well.

- A heavy extra-large 12 inch *cast iron, copper or anodized stainless steel chef's pan with lid* for sautéing or quickly cooking sauce ingredients in olive oil at a high temperature. Use this pan to finish-off the pasta with the sauce. Copper and non-stick skillets are fine as well.

- *Pasta ladles with "fingers"* to grasp pasta in the water or for serving pasta. Heavy plastic, wood, or steel will do fine. Also *stirring spoons*, preferably wooden.

- *Knives*- small paring knives and one large, heavy carving knife; both used for mincing and dicing ingredients.

- *Garlic press*- a really great way to have finely minced garlic that explodes with flavor.

- *Cheese grater, metal*- to grate the fresh cheese directly on the individual servings or for grating ahead of time. TIP: Also use it to grate carrots and other finely minced vegetables into your sauce.

5

- *Blender/Food Processor or Food Mill*- for pureeing tomatoes into a smooth sauce, blending sauces or herbs.

- *Large Italian style serving bowl with pasta bowl set*- available in most department stores. The large serving bowl makes for an eye-pleasing presentation with your favorite pasta dish.

- *Electric steamer* - I have an electric steamer that is fantastic for fish, vegetables, rice etc.

Multi-domed *Trullo* house.

HERBS
(Aromatici)

Fresh or dried herbs play a key part in Italian cooking. Subtle blending of herbs into a delightful marriage with other ingredients imparts a distinct but not overpowering flavor to dishes. If you are not inclined to grow or buy fresh herbs at your local market, dried herbs will do reconstituted in the sauce. Use smaller amounts of dried herbs because in a desiccated state herbs are more concentrated.

- Italian flat-leaf parsley (**prezzemolo**) or curly parsley is used in more Italian dishes than even oregano or basil. The Italian parsley has a more pungent flavor and is one of the key ingredients in any seafood-based sauce, the classic *marinara*, and the *aglio/oglio* (olive oil and garlic) sauce. A member of the carrot family, Italian flat-leaf parsley resembles carrot leaves when sprouting.

- Basil (**basilico**) has become popular from its use in the pesto sauce but the most basic and flavorful tomato-based sauce is comprised of nothing more than fresh tomatoes passed through a food mill combined with basil torn into small pieces, and olive oil. Fresh basil should be torn to prevent bruising. Basil being a member of the mint family has an even more pungent taste than parsley and its aroma is heavenly. In Naples it is placed in ceramic or terracotta jars around the exterior of the home not only for the aroma but to fend off mosquitoes. Basil along with other fresh herbs can be stored in the refrigerator in plastic bags.

- Rosemary (**rosmarino**) has a piney-flavor and best compliments dishes with meat or mushrooms. In Italy, chicken roasted on the spit is basted in a butter/olive oil rosemary sauce. It is most easily procured dried but rosemary shrubs are hardy enough to plant in your garden even in northern climes.

- Oregano (**origano**) or wild marjoram is the familiar "pizza" herb. Best used to impart a tangy flavor to tomato-based dishes *"alla pizzaiolo"* or pizza maker's style.

- Mint (**mento**) is used with meat or vegetables (lamb and zucchini).

- Sage (**salvia**) grayish, green aromatic leaves used widely in Northern Italy in meats but also excellent with butter and drizzled over any pasta.

- Thyme (**timo**)- another member of the mint family, thyme is excellent on vegetable and poultry dishes.

Below: The Simeone family in front of their *Trullo* house. Christian symbols adorn the dome of the *Trullo* house. These symbols at one time were thought to ward off the *"malocchio"* or evil eye.

CHEESE
(Formaggi)

Cheese is an integral part of Italian cuisine. Cheese is grated over pasta from fresh rounds or eaten after a main course in wedges. The most renowned and versatile of Italian cheese is the *Parmigiano-Reggiano* from the Po Valley farming and agriculture region of *Reggio Emilia*. It is normally aged about three years and is identified by the distinctive stamp on the rind. We know the American grated brand simply as Parmesan. Italians pride themselves in having the most flavorful cheeses and would never settle for the poor quality single sliced and other tasteless processed cheeses we find in our supermarkets. Each region in Italy has its own distinctive cheese. In the Northern part of Italy more cow-derived soft and hard cheeses are found; in the Southern regions sheep's milk cheese such as *pecorino* known as Romano cheese here, is more common along with water-buffalo *mozzarella* cheese in the *Campagnia* region around Naples, and goat cheeses. I recently called my cousin in Italy and he was in the countryside making goat and sheep cheese. I was fortunate to have friends; the Fusari's, of *Mantova* in *Reggio Emilia*, who produce *Reggiano-Parmigiano*. They would serve whole wedges with *cotechino* sausage, *salumi*, and *prosciutto*, washed down with fresh, dry, *Lambrusco*, the bubbly red regional wine. Fortunately, these cheeses are showing up more frequently in regular grocery store chains here in the USA. Underlined cheeses below are indispensable in the Italian kitchen.

- Asiago: Produced in the foothills of the Dolomites, originally from sheep's milk, now from cows. Aged, it becomes sharper and is used for grating. Very common in Northern Italy and where I lived in Thiene near the Dolomite Mountains.

- Baita Friulli: An Alpine cows' milk cheese that's firm enough to grate but mild enough to snack on.

- Bel Paese: Sweet, buttery and semi-soft, this is a modern cheese, invented in the 20th century. Its name means "beautiful country." Often served with wine or fruit, it also melts well.

- Caciocavallo: A hard cheese made from cows' milk, formed into a ball and tied. Especially popular in Sicily, it has a mild taste and melts well.

- Cacioricotta di Puglia: A tasty young sheep's milk cheese with a soft, creamy texture that's ideal for cooking and for grating. Similar to *Pecorino-Romano*. My cousins in *Puglia* make this cheese and age it on shelves in their *Trulli* houses.

- Caprini: Goats milk cheese- *"capra"* means goat. Formed in small molds usually eaten fresh. Aged in regions like my Apulia it is hard and grated on pasta like *pecorino* cheese.

- Crescenza: A fresh, rindless cheese, made of cows' milk. It has a mild luxurious taste.

- <u>Fior di Latte</u>: (flowers of milk) A soft cows' milk cheese with about two week's shelf life. It has the same consistency and taste as *mozzarella di bufala* and is more commonplace than mozzarella as a cheese entrée'.

- Fontina: From Valle d'Aosta, a straw-colored cheese with a thin brown rind. Made of cows' milk.

- <u>Gorgonzola</u>: Pungent, sharp and creamy, the Italian blue cheese.

- Grana Padano: A hard cows' milk cheese, similar in taste, appearance and use to Parmigiano-Reggiano. It is essentially another type of *Parmigiano* cheese.

- <u>Mascarpone</u>: Ivory-colored, fresh cheese with a velvety texture. Served with fruit or in the elaborate dessert called *tiramisu*. It is much like our <u>cream cheese</u>.

- <u>Mozzarella</u>: A pale melting cheese that also is sold smoked and called *"affumicata"*. *Scamorza* is a regional variant. Fresh *"mozzarella di bufala"* is increasingly common; it is softer, whiter and more perishable that the more familiar cheese. *"Mozzarella di bufala"* is found solely in the marshes outside of Naples strangely where the *Napolitani* like to picnic. It is the original cheese used on pizza's and is soft, delicate cheese unlike the hard tasteless version sold in our supermarkets. Made of water buffalo's milk.

- <u>Parmigiano Reggiano:</u> Considered the king of cheeses in Italy, its production is rigidly controlled. Sold in huge cylinders and usually aged about 3 years, it is a superb grating cheese. In Italy, paper-thin shavings often are served on salads or eaten as wedges after the main course.

- <u>Pecorino di Puglia:</u> *"Pecora"* means sheep and this is the most famous of sheep's-milk cheese. Hard and grainy with a pleasantly sharp taste, this is a table and grating cheese. *Pecorino* is found in most regions and the name *pecorino* followed by the region's name, e.g., *Sardo* for Sardinia identifies a regional variation or *Romano* from Rome is a more common variety.

- <u>Provolone</u>: An uncooked, smooth, pale cheese with a mild taste, made in the tip of the Italian boot. Size varies from small, pear-shaped packages to 200-pounders.

- <u>Ricotta</u>: A fresh white cheese, slightly grainy and mild. Its name means re-cooked and it often is the by-product of other cheese-making processes. *Ricotta salata* is salted and drained so it becomes firmer and more compact, somewhat like Greek feta but not as salty.

- Robiola: A soft, disk-shaped fresh cows' milk cheese with a faint, pleasant, acidic tang. It goes well with fruit.

- Taleggio: A square cheese with a golden rind and fine, creamy flavor.

Typical agricultural landscape around Cisternino. *Trulli* houses dot the countryside evoking a fairly-tale like atmosphere. This *Trullo* house is used during the *raccolto* or the fall harvest of crops.

Distant and almost mystical *Trullo* farmhouse.

What to stock: Condiments
(Condimenti)

Using condiments is the most effective means to flavor your sauces. In Italy overwhelming tomato sauces are practically unheard of. In most all restaurants and *tratorrie* you will be served your spaghetti, for example, with a small mound of sauce in the middle of the serving. The true delight in eating the pasta is the delicate blend of a flavored sauce with the "*al dente*" noodle. The list below is not totally comprehensive by all means, as there are hundreds of condiments used to flavor sauces. If you stock up on one or two of each item in the standard sized packages, bottles, or containers they are normally sold in, you will have a properly stocked Italian kitchen *(cucina italiana)*. Remember to buy the herbs and basic dried and fresh cheeses to your liking in the previous section as well. I can remember to this day the wonderful aroma of my grandfather Pentassuglia's kitchen. The pungent yet pleasant aroma of *pecorino-romano* cheese wafted through his pantry, which had the glass beads hanging in the entrance as a partition to his kitchen.

- **Anchovies**- Several anchovy filets dissolved in a sauce are low in fat and impart a delicate seafood flavor to dishes. Used mainly in tomato-based sauces with parsley and capers.

- **Artichoke Hearts**- canned in water or bottled.

- **Asparagus**- canned or fresh.

- **Balsamic and red wine vinegar**- keep both types on hand. You don't have to have the most expensive types but aged balsamic vinegar is an exceptional condiment.

- **Bouillon cubes**- how many people do you know today in our rushed society have the time to lord over pots of boiling chicken bones to make the perfect broth which subsequently has to be stored in the refrigerator in a huge pot? My cousins in Apulia use high quality bouillon cubes as a method to add zest and flavor to a dish. Adding a bouillon cube to a tomato or cream sauce adds a flavor boost that many homemade broths can't compare with. You can buy beef, chicken, vegetable and fish bouillon cubes at all major grocery stores. **Secret tip: The brand I prefer is Knorr'®s because the cubes are flavorful, large and very soft.**

- **Capers**- tiny, tart, green spheres which are the buds of a Mediterranean shrub. You can buy bottled in brine in small narrow jars. Use with seafood dishes and mushroom sauces.

- **Cinnamon**- used in cream sauces and béchamel (**besciamella**) sauces to impart an exotic, eastern flavor.

- **Canned Clams**- minced or chopped, to make quick *"vongole"* sauce, using the liquid in the can as well. <u>Also stock a bottle of clam juice found on most grocery stores to add zest to seafood dishes.</u>

- **Garlic & Onions**- Italians like the sweet red or white onions over others. Keep fresh garlic cloves on-hand. Mince the garlic using a garlic press.

- **Hot pepper flakes**- for adding an *"arrabbiata"* (literally angry) or hot and spicy flavor to tomato based sauces. Used mainly in Southern Italy. You can also use fresh or dried whole red peppers or *peperoncini*.

- **Leeks**- fresh leeks impart a mild-onion flavor.

- **Lemons**- used to marinade vegetables and meat. The rind is grated and combined with parsley to make *"gremolata"*, a condiment used with meat, fish and pasta dishes. Lemon juice is also used in sauces.

- **Mushrooms** (funghi)- three types commonly available in grocery stores are button, *Cremini* (dark, brown button-type) and *Portabella* (thick, large brown caps). Dried *Porcini* are optimal when reconstituted in water but are expensive.

- **Mussels, smoked**- *"Le Cozze"* are wonderful fresh but if you are in a hurry, smoked mussels can be added to pasta for flavoring.

- **Nutmeg**- used like Cinnamon in cream and béchamel sauces.

- **Olives**- buy small Gaeta olives, from a seaside region north of Naples, or the Greek Kalamata olives, which are very tart, and almond shaped. Green olives from *Cerignola* in *Puglia* are fantastic and mild in taste. Most olives are available at delicatessens and some major grocery chains.

- **Olive Oil**- extra-virgin is the best, made from the first cold pressing of olives. The aroma and taste is more important than the color. Store in cool, dark recesses in the kitchen. A good olive should have a rich nutty taste.

- **Peas**- fresh or frozen, peas are found in a variety of pasta dishes.

- **Pesto**- a Ligurian paste made of basil, pine nuts, garlic, *pecorino* or *parmigiano* cheese and olive oil. Use as a condiment on pasta by itself or marinade meat and fish before grilling.

- **Pine Nuts**- toast pine nuts in a small skillet until golden brown. Use with vegetable sauces to add a nutty, crunchy texture to your dishes.

- **Roasted Red Peppers**- take red peppers in season; char the outside skins until black on a gas stove or broiler. Cool and peel the carbonized peel, cut in strips and marinade in red wine vinegar and olive oil. Place in a sterile container and keep refrigerated. (or buy commercially in jars)

- **Salmon, smoked**- found in any seafood department of grocery stores, smoked salmon is sold in packages of 8 to 16 ounces. Used in sauces with vodka and cream sauce or in tomato-based dishes.

- **Sea Salt**- use quality ground sea salt to enhance your dishes.

- **Spinach**- frozen chopped or fresh spinach is used as stuffing or combined with other vegetables, meats, and fish.

- **Sun-Dried Tomatoes**- found in grocery stores in the fresh produce sections in jars marinated in olive oil they are quite expensive. You can do it yourself for a fraction of the price. Use a dehydrator or take a cookie sheet placing about 2-3 pounds of plum or Roma tomatoes sliced in half lengthwise on the sheets. Place them in the oven overnight at a very, very low temperature selection; (Warm 150 degrees). In the morning they will be shriveled, dried, and slightly caramelized giving them a pulpy texture and slightly sweet taste. Store the tomatoes in small bottles with extra-virgin olive oil in the refrigerator. These tomatoes are great in cold pasta dishes or with cream sauces and roasted red peppers.

- **Tuna**- Italian canned tuna in olive oil is the best if you can find it.

- **Worcestershire sauce**- discovered recently by Italian chefs and used to flavor sauce in place of veal stock.

Other items to stock in your Italian Kitchen
(Beans, Vegetables, Dairy Products, Meats, and Fish)

Here are some staples needed in the kitchen to prepare the pasta recipes in this book. Some of the condiments listed previously would also be staples, such as peas and tuna, but they are used often to flavor sauces, hence they were listed primarily as condiments. You can purchase the staples listed below in varying quantities, but try to keep at least one ration of each in the refrigerator or cupboard. For items annotated as fresh, buy as needed.

Beans- Keep plenty of beans on hand for quick "*pasta e fagiola*" meals. *Ceci* or *garbanzo* and *fava* pureed with olive oil, parsley and garlic make a super peasant fare over pasta. Other beans such as "*cannellini*" or white kidney beans, red kidney beans, pintos, great northern beans, and green beans can be used as well.

Vegetables (Verdure)- Here is a fairly comprehensive list of vegetables to regularly keep on hand in order to prepare the recipes in this book. You may prefer other vegetables. These are not in any particular order.

⇒ artichokes (canned in water or in jars packed in oil)
⇒ arugula
⇒ asparagus (canned or in season)
⇒ basil, fresh
⇒ broccoli
⇒ eggplant
⇒ zucchini
⇒ spinach (frozen or fresh)
⇒ carrots
⇒ celery
⇒ cauliflower
⇒ canned Plum, Roma or San Marzano tomatoes, crushed- buy 28 ounce or 1 pound, 12 ounce cans by the case
⇒ canned Plum, Roma or San Marzano tomatoes, whole- buy 28 ounce or 1 pound, 12 ounce cans by the case
⇒ diced tomatoes- buy in 14 ½ ounce cans by the case
⇒ tomato paste -2 small cans
⇒ tomato puree-several cans
⇒ onions
⇒ fennel
⇒ garlic
⇒ mixed greens- canned "Glory" brand; use in recipes as a substitute for spinach, arugula, turnip greens etc.
⇒ mushrooms-button, *cremini, porcini, portabella*
⇒ peas (frozen)
⇒ parsley, Italian flat-leaf

⇒ Swiss chard (seasonal)

Dairy Products (Prodotti di Latte)

* whole or skim milk
* cheese listed in the other section
* whipping or heavy cream- several pints
* butter or margarine

Meats and Sausages (Carne e Salumi)

◊ *pancetta*- or thick slab American bacon, Canadian bacon, or pork jowl
◊ *prosciutto*- Italian salt-cured ham, *San Daniele* or *Parma* (more expensive)
◊ *prosciutto cotto*- cooked ham or a good quality American cooked ham slices
◊ salami
◊ chicken or turkey breast fillets
◊ pork fillets
◊ veal fillets
◊ lamb
◊ ground beef
◊ top round or flank steak for *Braciole*
◊ Italian sweet sausage
◊ beef roast cut or thick London broil, chuck roast for the true *Bolognese & Ragu* sauce

Fish (Pesce)

♦ *calamari* (frozen or fresh squid)
♦ shrimp or prawns (frozen or fresh)
♦ anchovies (canned)
♦ mussels (fresh)
♦ scallops (frozen or fresh)
♦ clams (fresh or minced canned) *Gorton's* ® brand
♦ smoked salmon (packaged)
♦ tuna, white albacore packed in water
♦ lobster (frozen or fresh)
♦ white fish fillets such as haddock, flounder etc.

Typical street in Cisternino. Cisternino is known for its vaulted arches and whitewashed buildings.

About Pasta

Pasta makers are great if you have a quality machine and know how to use it, but most of us simply don't have the time to prepare the dough, process it and clean the machine. With hectic work schedules, not much time is allocated to meal preparation so we want pasta to be ready-made, either fresh or dried commercial *pasta asciutta* we find in supermarkets. I noticed that semolina flour is hard to find and expensive so that you can actually buy pasta in the grocery stores cheaper than you can make it yourself.

In Italy each region has its own particular shape. In Apulia where my family hails from, "little ears" or *orrechiette* are popular. It is made by a thumb imprint in the dough with a little twist to give the pasta its final concave form.

Each neighborhood in Italy still has the little "Ma and Pop" grocery store operations although *superingrosso's* or "wholesale" type buying stores and chain retailers such as Standa and UPIM have been around for decades. The local pasta shop is called a "*pastaufficio*" or literally the pasta shop. Italians use both commercial *pasta asciutta* and fresh pasta purchased daily. Italians have small refrigerators for two reasons (1) they insist on fresh ingredients without chemicals (2) electric current is cost prohibitive in Italy, having a large refrigerator would cost a small fortune monthly and this is the same reason air conditioners are scarce.

Italians normally have a three-course meal daily, but more at lunch when it is subsidized by the government in a *mensa* or *cafeteria* if you are a *statale* or government employee. Schoolchildren come home for lunch as well as the self-employed. The first course (*primo piatto)* of the three-course meal is usually pasta or soup, followed by a *secondo piatto* of meat or fish and several vegetables; the *terzo piatto* is cheese and /or fruit in season. Each course could be served with a different type of wine. Italians keep pasta portions small about 2-3 ounces per serving since it's just the first course of a well-balanced meal. There aren't many overweight Italians since their lifestyle includes well-proportioned balanced diets with walking as a daily activity.

Pasta should never swim in tomato sauce. In Italy delicate sauces of vegetables, herbs, meats and fish nap the pasta so one can enjoy the *al dente* pasta and subtle flavoring of the sauce. Most tomato sauces are made of fresh tomatoes passed through a food mill or sieve. In general about a pint of sauce is adequate to moisten one pound of pasta. Here are some tips to preparing pasta like a native:

- Not less than six quarts of water per pound of pasta cooked.
- Salt can be added but is optional. Sea salt is preferred.
- Never put oil in the water; it coats the pasta making a barrier so the sauce can't permeate the pasta with its flavor.

- Don't break up long types of pasta such as linguine because when served it will look like leftovers (*Conti corte e tagliatelle lunghe*) or small bills and long pasta as the saying in Italy goes.
- Bring water to a boil before adding pasta.
- Add whole quantity of pasta at the same time for a consistent cooking time.
- Better to undercook a little than overcook. If pasta is undercooked you can finish it of by letting it simmer in the sauce for a few minutes. It will absorb the sauce and taste delightful.
- Use a wooden spoon to push the pasta around.
- Use a wooden, metal or plastic pasta ladle with teeth to stir frequently with and transfer drained pasta.
- Don't overcook the pasta; it should always be "*al dente*" or firm to the teeth. Depending on the density and size of the pasta cooking times will vary. Taste test it every few minutes and when it sticks to the wall it truly is ready!
- Drain and mix with the sauce immediately. Do not rinse it with cold water as it will become cold and will be impossible to re-heat without ruination.
- Place on a huge platter with herb garnish and sprinkle with a little cheese if the recipe calls for it.
- Cheese doesn't go well with fish based sauce and pasta dishes. There are exceptions however.
- I prefer extra-virgin olive oil for all cooking requiring olive oil. Some say the extra-virgin olive oil should only be used in salads but like many things it is a matter of personal taste. Use the oil as needed or (qb) quanto basta in Italian.

Cousin Antonetta making "orecchiette" (Cisternino, Italy 2004)

About Sauce

There are some basic sauces, which can be built upon to make many variations of sauce for your quick pasta meals. The Italians avoid commercially prepared sauces in all but extreme situations (feeding a screaming toddler or teenager) because commercial sauces have fat, conservatives, corn oil, sugar and other chemicals that don't belong in sauce or in your body. In the time it takes to boil the water you can even prepare tomato-based sauces because Italians like fresh sauces cooked in twenty minutes or less with fresh or canned tomatoes. Only a few traditional sauces require cooking time of an hour or more. I like to keep a case of crushed or whole canned tomatoes on-hand when I can find them on sale. There is no fat, sugar or other additives in canned whole or crushed tomatoes. I prefer using canned Italian plum tomatoes to all other types of tomatoes to maintain authenticity and flavor.

Another preferred way to make sauce is to take Roma or San Marzano plum tomatoes which are very fleshy with few seeds and blanch them for a few minutes in boiling water. Remove the tomatoes from the water with a slotted spoon and gently remove the peel with a paring knife. Chop the tomatoes finely and gently simmer for no more than 20 minutes for a colorful red sauce.

Two terms that I use often that I want to clarify are sauté and simmer. By sauté (FR. sauter: to jump). In Italian we say *"saltare"* which also means to jump because the heat is so intense the ingredients seem to jump in the pan or *padella*.. I mean in the French sense to cook a meat or vegetable in a strong heat in oil, fat or butter. By simmer I mean to cook gently over a medium to low heat. The Italian term for simmer is *soffriggere* which means to lightly fry.

My favorite way to flavor any sauce without adding fat is to use good bouillon such as Knorr®'s of any variety. You can use a brand of your choice; just make sure the cubes are large and soft. The bouillon added whole will add a concentrated chicken, beef, vegetable or fish flavor to your sauce. In preparing drier sauces, use bouillon dissolved in a cup of water in your microwave or on the stove in a saucepan. Other flavorings include the aforementioned herbs, capers, anchovies, Worcestershire sauce, steamed vegetables etc. As mentioned earlier, undercook your pasta by a minute or so and finish cooking it in your saucepan or sauté pan. In this manner the pasta will absorb your sauce instead of water.

Besciamella or **Béchamel White Sauce-** In many of my recipes I will make a white sauce used mostly in Northern Italy in Emilia-Romagna. It is difficult to find good heavy cream in American grocery stores such as the **Parmalat** brand **Chef Panna** that I was accustomed to in Italy for making a luscious rich cream sauce. I will often use a *besciamella* sauce instead, although because of the flour it has a different taste and texture when compared to a cream sauce. My *besciamella* is different because I use a bouillon cube in the early stages with the butter and flour, therefore no salt is required in my sauce and I like the flavor imparted by the bouillon cube.

Basic Besciamella
Preparation Time: 6 minutes

Ingredients:

* 1/2 stick of sweet butter
* 1/2 cup of all purpose flour
* 4 cups or 2 pints of hot milk or half & half
* salt and white pepper to taste
* 1 Knorr®'s chicken bouillon cube
* pinch of nutmeg and cinnamon (optional)

Melt the butter in a saucepan. Stir in the flour and mix with a wooden spoon over low heat. Break up the bouillon cube in the mixture. Continue stirring for about 2 minutes until there is a lump or *roux* making sure not to let the flour/butter mixture burn. Add the pre-heated milk slowly (from the microwave) whisking (with a wire-whisk) continuously until the texture is smooth. Turn up the heat to high stirring continuously for 4 minutes until the mixture starts to boil and thickens. Quickly remove from heat and set aside. Add the pinch each of nutmeg and cinnamon. Add a few tablespoons or more of *parmigiano* cheese and mix if you wish.

Basic Recipes (Le Ricette)

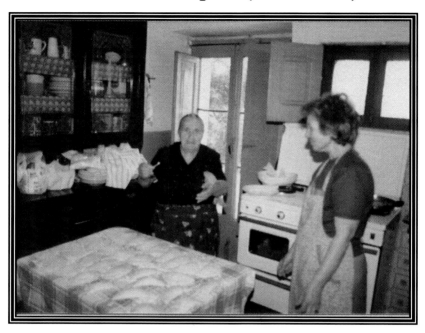

My late Zia Felice and cousin making tasty "*Panzerotti*" meat, cheese and vegetable filled pastries in her country house in Cisternino Italy.

Panzerotti:

2 pounds of flour	1 tablespoon of salt
1 tablespoon of sugar	3 teaspoons of extra-virgin olive oil
1 package of baker's yeast	½ cup of dry white wine
4 balls of fresh mozzarella	1 large can of whole plum tomatoes, diced
1 small potato, shredded	

Take the flour and make a well on a board adding the sugar, salt, oil, wine, shredded potato and yeast in the middle. Add warm water and work the dough until it is soft and elastic. Cover with a warm towel for 30 minutes to allow it to rise. Re-work the dough with your hands again and form dough balls the size of oranges. Re-cover the dough with a warm wet towel and allow it to rise again for 30 minutes. In a mixing bowl, shred the mozzarella and mix with the diced tomatoes. At this point take a rolling pin and flatten out the orange-shaped balls into disks. Fill one side of each disk with a few tablespoons of the filling. Fold the dough over the mixture making a half-moon shape. Use the end of a fork to close the half-moon shapes. Fry the Panzerotti in abundant hot oil until golden brown. Place on a plate with paper towels and serve hot.

Spaghetti Aglio ed Oglio- The most basic sauce and one that is the basis for several famous variations. Take care not to burn the garlic. The oil should be hot enough to infuse the flavor of the garlic into the olive oil by sautéing. Variations using Italian flat-leaf parsley, basil or fresh oregano change the character of the dish to an entirely different taste. Using freshly ground pepper from a pepper mill adds extra zest to the dish.

Preparation Time: 20 minutes

Ingredients:

- 1 pound of Spaghetti
- 4 large garlic cloves, minced
- 4 tablespoons of olive oil or as needed (qb) quanto basta in Italian
- 1/2 cup of fresh Italian flat-leaf parsley, chopped
- a pinch of hot pepper flakes or *peperoncini*, chopped
- salt and pepper to taste

Fill a 10-quart saucepan with water over high heat for the pasta. Add the pasta after the water reaches a boil, approximately 10 minutes before the final preparation of the recipe. Add the olive oil to a pre-heated saucepan. *Soffriggere* or lightly fry the garlic, hot pepper flakes and half of the parsley until the garlic takes on a little color but is not browned. Discard or leave the garlic to your liking. Combine the drained *al dente* pasta with the saucepan ingredients and cook for an additional minute. Garnish with the remaining parsley. Add salt and ground pepper to taste.

variations: 1) add more than a pinch of hot pepper flakes to the garlic and oil 2) replace parsley with basil or oregano 3) or sauté two anchovy fillets with the garlic.

Spaghetti al Pomodoro I- Your basic tomato sauce prepared very easily with several variations. You can make it entirely fat-free by excluding any oils or lard but the traditional sauces use olive oil and in Naples or the *Campagnia* region lard is used. When prepared with parsley this is the true *"Marinara"* from *"Marinaio"* or sailor's sauce because it can be prepared quickly for hungry patrons and seafood can be added (such as octopus or *polipi*.). Parsley marries perfectly with seafood.

Preparation Time: 30 minutes

Ingredients:

- 1 pound of Spaghetti
- 1 (28) ounce or 1 pound 12 ounce can of whole Italian plum tomatoes, diced or crushed tomatoes
- 4 tablespoons of olive oil or as needed (qb) quanto basta in Italian
- 1/4 cup of fresh Italian flat-leaf parsley, chopped
- 3 whole garlic cloves, minced
- 1 Knorr®'s vegetable bouillon cube (optional)
- salt and pepper to taste

Fill a 10-quart saucepan with water over high heat for the pasta. Add the pasta after the water reaches a boil, approximately 10 minutes before the final preparation of the recipe. Pre-heat a saucepan over high heat, adding the olive oil when hot. *Soffriggere* or lightly fry the garlic and half of the parsley in the olive oil for a few minutes. Discard the garlic if desired. Add the tomatoes with liquid and bouillon cube to the saucepan. Simmer all ingredients together for 20 minutes. Combine the drained *al dente* pasta with the saucepan ingredients and cook for an additional minute. Transfer the completed dish to a serving platter or bowl. Garnish with the remaining parsley. Serve grated *parmigiano* or *pecorino* cheese apart.

variation: use 2 tablespoons of dried basil or 1/3 cup of torn basil.

Spaghetti al Pomodoro II- A tomato sauce that has a Northern Italian influence. When meat is added to this version it becomes a *Ragu'* sauce characteristic of the *Emilia-Romagna* region or the city of Bologna, renown for its superb meat-based *Ragu'* and *Bolognese* sauces.

Preparation Time: 30 minutes

Ingredients:

- 1 pound of Spaghetti
- 1 (28) ounce or 1 pound 12 ounce can of whole Italian plum tomatoes, diced or crushed tomatoes
- 4 tablespoons of olive oil or as needed (qb) quanto basta in Italian
- 1/4 cup of fresh Italian flat-leaf parsley, chopped
- pinch of rosemary
- 1 tablespoon of thyme
- 3 whole garlic cloves, minced
- 1/2 of a small carrot, minced
- 1/4 stalk of celery, minced
- 1/2 of a medium-sized sweet onion, diced
- 1/2 cup of dry white wine
- 1 Knorr®'s vegetable bouillon cube (optional)

Fill a 10-quart saucepan with water over high heat for the pasta. Add the pasta after the water reaches a boil, approximately 10 minutes before the final preparation of the recipe. Pre-heat a saucepan over medium heat, adding the olive oil when hot. *Soffriggere* or lightly fry the garlic, onions, carrots, celery and half of the parsley in the olive oil for a few minutes. Add the tomatoes with liquid, the crushed bouillon cube, wine, thyme, rosemary and remaining parsley. Simmer all ingredients together for 20 minutes. Combine the drained *al dente* pasta with the saucepan ingredients and cook for an additional minute. Transfer the completed dish to a serving platter or bowl. Serve with grated *parmigiano* or *pecorino* cheese apart.

variation: use 2 tablespoons of dried basil or 1/3 cup of torn basil.

Pasta al Ragu'- Add meat to the preceding Pomodoro II sauce and a classic Ragu' is rendered. You don't have to cook it for hours and hours for it to be delicious. One main difference in Italy is that fewer tomatoes are used in this dish creating a more dense sauce. Later I will show you how to make the traditional Sunday feast *"Bolognese"* sauce, which is the only recipe that would take several hours to prepare.

Preparation Time: 30 minutes

Ingredients:

- 1 pound box of Ziti
- 1 (28) ounce or 1 pound, 12 ounce can of crushed tomatoes
- 1 (14) ounce can of diced tomatoes or canned plum tomatoes
- 2 tablespoons of tomato paste
- 4 tablespoons olive oil or as needed (qb) quanto basta in Italian
- 1/4 cup of fresh Italian flat-leaf parsley, chopped
- pinch of rosemary
- pinch of thyme
- 1 tablespoon of dried, crumbled sage
- 2 bay leaves
- 1 tablespoon marjoram (optional)
- 3 whole garlic cloves, minced
- 1/2 of a small carrot, minced
- 1/4 stalk of celery, minced
- 1/2 of a medium-sized onion, diced
- 1/2 pound of ground chuck or beef
- 1/2 pound of ground pork
- 1/2 cup of dry, white or red wine
- 1 Knorr®'s beef bouillon cube

Fill a 10-quart saucepan with water over high heat for the pasta. Add the pasta after the water reaches a boil, approximately 10 minutes before the final preparation of the recipe. Pre-heat a saucepan over medium heat, adding the olive oil when hot. *Soffriggere* or lightly fry the garlic, onions, carrots, and celery and all of the herbs (parsley, sage, rosemary, bay leaves, thyme, and marjoram) for a few minutes. Add the ground beef, and pork frying until browned (*rosolare*). Add the tomatoes, the bouillon cubes, wine and tomato paste to the meat and herbs in the saucepan. Simmer all ingredients together for 25 minutes. Combine drained *al dente* pasta with the saucepan ingredients and cook for an additional minute. Transfer the completed dish to a serving platter or bowl. Top with grated *parmigiano* or *pecorino* cheese. Serve with grated cheese apart as well.

variation: use 2 tablespoons of dried basil or 1/3 cup of torn basil.

Aunt Catherine (left) and my wife Evie in the main piazza of Cisternino. Cisternino was once a fortress for the Normans, Frederick II of Swabia, the Venetians, the House of Anjou from Naples and the Aragonese Spanish. The entire town is whitewashed and kept spotlessly clean.

One of four towers in Cisternino reinforced and refurbished by the Spanish in the 15th century as seen from the outside.

Spaghetti Puttanesca- This aromatic dish has the essence of Southern Italy's Adriatic sea. It is based upon the true Marinara sauce or Pomodoro I sauce described earlier. This dish is served at *festa's* or celebrations. Known in Naples as a *puttanesca* sauce because Harlots could make it quickly between clients.

Preparation Time: 30 minutes

Ingredients:

- 1 pound of Spaghetti
- 1 (28 ounce) or 1 pound 12 ounce can of crushed tomatoes
- 1 (14) ounce can of diced tomatoes
- 2 tablespoons of olive oil or as needed (qb) quanto basta in Italian
- 1/4 cup of fresh Italian flat-leaf parsley, chopped
- 4 whole garlic cloves, minced
- 1/2 of a medium-sized sweet onion, diced
- 2 tablespoons of capers
- 1/4 cup of black *gaeta* olives, pitted and chopped
- 4 flat anchovy fillets (canned) or a teaspoon of anchovy paste
- 2 tablespoons of clam juice (from jar) or
- 1/2 of a Knorr®'s fish bouillon cube (optional)

Fill a 10-quart saucepan with water over high heat for the pasta. Add the pasta after the water reaches a boil, approximately 10 minutes before the final preparation of the recipe. Pre-heat a saucepan over medium heat, adding the olive oil when the pan is hot. *Soffriggere* or lightly fry the anchovies, garlic, onion and the parsley in the olive oil until the anchovy fillets dissolve. Add the capers, olives and tomatoes to the saucepan. Simmer all ingredients together for 15 minutes. Add the clam juice or bouillon and cook an additional 3-5 minutes. Combine the *al dente* pasta with the saucepan ingredients and cook for an additional minute. Transfer the completed dish to a serving platter or bowl. Serve with grated *pecorino* cheese apart.

variation: add hot pepper flakes for an "*arrabbiata*" zing or chopped roasted red pepper.

Vegetable-Based Sauces
(Le Verdure)

Cisternino and the surrounding Valley of Itria abound in agricultural produce. Lemon, almond, olive, peach, cherry and fig trees abound. Vegetables include artichokes, arugula, cauliflower, broccolini, cherry tomatoes, zucchini, eggplant, onions (*lampascioni* or wild onions), garlic, capers (actually a bush) peppers, fava beans, ceci beans, peas and potatoes just to name a few. Subsequently many of the pasta dishes have vegetable-based condiments served with rich and tasty extra-virgin olive oil of the region.

Penne con Broccoli e Cavolfiore (Broccoli & Cauliflower Florets)-
Vegetable dishes are popular in my region of Apulia. Once considered peasant
food for the lack of meat these healthful dishes are now in vogue because they are
low in fat and high in natural minerals and vitamins. Little wonder my Grandfather
lived into his nineties!

Preparation Time: 30 minutes

Ingredients:

- 1 pound of Penne
- 1/2 of a fresh firm head of broccoli, pared into florets
- 1/2 of a fresh firm head of cauliflower, pared into florets
- 4 tablespoons of olive oil
- 1/4 cup of fresh Italian flat-leaf parsley, chopped
- 4 whole garlic cloves, minced
- 1small sweet onion, diced
- 1 Knorr®'s vegetable bouillon cube
- 1/2 cup of dry white wine (optional) or water

Fill a 10-quart saucepan with water over high heat for the pasta. Add the pasta after
the water reaches a boil, approximately 10 minutes before the final preparation of
the recipe. Steam the broccoli and cauliflower in a steamer no more than 10
minutes (cooked yet firm) or steam in the bottom of a 10-quart saucepan with few
cups of water. Pre-heat a saucepan over medium heat, adding the olive oil when
hot. *Soffriggere* or lightly fry the garlic, onion and the parsley in the olive oil for a
few minutes. Discard the garlic if desired. Add 1/2 cup of water or white wine and
the crushed bouillon cube. Simmer until the bouillon cube is dissolved. Add the
broccoli and cauliflower florets and sauté with the other ingredients for 5 minutes.
Add a little (pasta) water if too dry. Combine or toss the *al dente* pasta with the
saucepan ingredients. Top with grated *pecorino* cheese. Transfer the completed
dish to a serving platter or bowl adding any remaining parsley as garnish.

variation: add hot pepper flakes for an "*arrabbiata*" zing.

Capellini all'Anita (Boscaiola Sauce) or Angel Hair pasta Anita style- This wonderful dish was prepared for me by a family friend with three children under four years of age, proof that good cooking and nutrition don't have to suffer because of an extremely hectic schedule. It evokes a *"boscaiola"* or "woodsy" flavor by combining mushrooms, capers, and sun-dried tomatoes.

Preparation Time: 30 minutes

Ingredients:

- 1 pound of Angel Hair pasta or thin Spaghetti
- 1/2 pound of fresh *portabella* mushrooms (or white button mushrooms if *portabella* aren't available)
- small package of dried *porcini* mushrooms (ask your grocer)
- 4 tablespoons of olive oil
- 1/4 cup of fresh Italian flat-leaf parsley, chopped
- 4 whole garlic cloves, minced
- 1/2 of a small sweet onion, diced
- 2 tablespoons of capers (bottled in brine)
- 1 cup of sun dried tomatoes
- 4 ounces of fresh baby spinach leaves
- 1/2 cup of pitted and sliced black olives
- 1 Knorr®'s vegetable bouillon cube
- 3 tablespoons of Italian balsamic vinegar
- 1/2 cup of dry white wine or water

Fill a 10-quart saucepan with water over high heat for the pasta. Add the pasta after the water reaches a boil, approximately 10 minutes before the final preparation of the recipe. Cook angel hair pasta only 4-5 minutes. Be careful not to overcook! Place the dried *porcini* mushrooms in a small bowl and barely cover them with lukewarm water for fifteen minutes. Chop the *portabella* mushrooms (already cleaned) into tiny pieces. Pre-heat a saucepan over medium heat, adding the olive oil when hot. *Soffriggere* or lightly fry the garlic, onion and half of the parsley in the olive oil for a few minutes. Add the *portabella* mushrooms and fry with the other ingredients for 10 minutes. Add 1/2 cup of water or white wine, bouillon cube, *porcini* mushrooms with liquid, spinach leaves and simmer until the bouillon is dissolved and <u>most</u> of the liquid evaporates. Add the capers, olives, sun-dried tomatoes, and the vinegar. Combine the *al dente* pasta with the saucepan ingredients. Transfer the completed dish to a serving platter or bowl adding the remaining parsley as garnish. Serve with grated *pecorino* or *parmigiano* cheese apart.

variations: 1) add hot pepper flakes for an *"arrabbiata"* zing. 2) add dried sage leaves with the sauté of garlic & olive oil in place of the parsley.

Farfalle Primavera- A *Primavera* can be any combination of vegetables that are on-hand. Use the steamer to prepare crisp vegetables and finish them off by sautéing with garlic, onions, and olive oil.

Preparation Time: 30 minutes

Ingredients:

- 1 pound of Farfalle (butterfly pasta)
- 1/2 pound of fresh *portabella* mushrooms (or white button mushrooms if *portabellas* aren't available), chopped
- 1 (2) ounce package of dried *porcini* mushrooms (ask your grocer)
- 1/4 head of fresh broccoli, pared and cleaned florets only
- 3 small zucchini, sliced
- 1 small eggplant, cubed
- 1 (28 ounce) or 1 pound 12 ounce can of crushed tomatoes
- 4 tablespoons of olive oil
- 1/4 cup of fresh Italian flat-leaf parsley, chopped
- 1 small sweet onion, diced
- 4 whole garlic cloves, minced
- 1 Knorr®'s vegetable bouillon cube
- 1/2 cup of dry white wine (optional) or water

Fill a 10-quart saucepan with water over high heat for the pasta. Add the pasta after the water reaches a boil, approximately 10 minutes before the final preparation of the recipe. Cook until *al dente*, and drain. Cut the vegetables as described above, place aside in cold water. Place the dried *porcini* mushrooms in a small bowl and barely cover with lukewarm water for 10 minutes. Pre-heat a saucepan over medium heat, adding the olive oil when hot. *Soffriggere* or lightly fry the garlic, onion and half of the parsley in the olive oil for a few minutes. Add the *portabella* mushrooms, eggplant and tomatoes and simmer with the other ingredients for 15 minutes. Add a little water if needed. Meanwhile steam the broccoli and sliced zucchini for 10 minutes in the steamer. Add the steamed vegetables, *porcini* mushrooms and liquid, and 1/2 cup of water or white wine and bouillon cube to the other already simmering vegetables. Simmer until the bouillon is dissolved. Combine the drained *al dente* pasta with the saucepan ingredients. Transfer the completed dish to a large serving bowl. Top with grated *pecorino* or *parmigiano* cheese and remaining parsley.

Ziti alle Melanzane (eggplant or aubergines)- Eggplant is becoming ever more popular for those who are diet conscious. Eggplant is a very versatile vegetable that is highly fibrous and has the consistency somewhat of meat without the cholesterol and fat. There are several types of eggplant, large and globular, Italian small and cylindrical, and the purple and white Chinese variation among others. Eggplant should be sliced or cubed and soaked in salt water, if time permits, for 30 minutes or so in a bowl with some weight on top to rid it of any bitterness. I've prepared it without soaking and it turns out fine. It can be boiled, baked, fried or steamed. If frying, the oil should be very hot initially to avoid excessive absorption by the eggplant of the oil and then the heat should be turned down after a few minutes so as not to burn the eggplant.

Preparation Time: 30 minutes

Ingredients:

- 1 pound of Ziti
- 1 pound of eggplant or 1 large eggplant, sliced
- 2 eggs, beaten
- 2 cups of flour
- 2 cups of grated *parmigiano* cheese
- 2 -3 cups of vegetable oil for frying

For the tomato sauce
- 1 (28 ounce) or 1 pound, 12 ounce can of crushed tomatoes
- 1 (14.5) ounce can of diced tomatoes
- 2 tablespoons of olive oil
- 1/4 cup of fresh Italian flat-leaf parsley, chopped
- 1/2 of a small sweet onion, diced
- 4 whole garlic cloves, minced
- 1 Knorr®'s vegetable bouillon cube
- 1/2 cup of dry white wine (optional) or water
- salt and pepper to taste

Fill a 10-quart saucepan with water over high heat for the pasta. Add the pasta after the water reaches a boil, approximately 10 minutes before the final preparation of the recipe.

For the sauce:
Pre-heat a saucepan over medium heat, adding the olive oil when hot. *Soffriggere* or lightly fry the garlic, onion and the parsley in the olive oil for a few minutes. Discard the garlic if desired. Add the tomatoes, white wine and the bouillon cube to the saucepan and simmer all of the ingredients together for 20 minutes.

For the eggplant:

After soaking the eggplant in water, pat dry, halve lengthwise and cut 1/4 inch thick lengthwise slices. Cut the 1/4-inch slices into 1-inch wide strips. If the eggplant is large cut the strips in half to about 3-4 inches long like French fries. Dip the strips in beaten egg and then a mixture of the flour and grated *parmigiano* cheese. Shake off excess flour. Pre-heat the vegetable oil in a large fry pan over high heat. Add the eggplant strips and fry until golden brown and floating. Remove with slotted spoon and dry off on a plate lined with a paper towel. Combine the drained *al dente* pasta with the tomato saucepan ingredients. Toss so the sauce coats the pasta. Transfer the pasta to a large serving bowl. Arrange the warm eggplant strips on top like spokes of a wheel. Top with grated *pecorino* or *parmigiano* cheese and a little parsley for garnish.

variations: 1) use 2 tablespoons dried basil or 1/3 cup of torn basil. Add hot pepper flakes for an "*arrabbiata*" zing. 2) Add a cup of *besciamella* sauce (pg. 22) to the finished dish, and then place the eggplant on top of the *besciamella* and pasta.

Country *Trullo* residence. Cisternino residents escape to their country *Trulli* houses during the hot summers.

Spaghetti con gli Zucchini- Green summer squash or zucchini is becoming ever more popular for those who are diet conscious. Use your vegetable steamer to make crisp little zucchini disks or sauté them in the saucepan. Don't over-steam the zucchini; it should be a vibrant green color.

Preparation Time: 30 minutes

Ingredients:

- 1 pound of Spaghetti
- 1/2 pound fresh zucchini or 4 medium sized zucchini
- 1 cup of bread crumbs
- 6 tablespoons of olive oil
- 1/4 cup of fresh Italian flat-leaf parsley, chopped
- 1 small sweet onion, diced
- 2 whole garlic cloves, minced
- 1 Knorr®'s vegetable or chicken bouillon cube
- 1/2 cup of water

Fill a 10-quart saucepan with water over high heat for the pasta. Add the pasta after the water reaches a boil, approximately 10 minutes before the final preparation of the recipe. Wash and scrub the zucchini and trim off the stem end. Slice the zucchini length-wise and half into 1/4 inch diameter strips. Pre-heat a saucepan over high heat adding half of the olive oil when hot. Add the garlic, onion, and parsley and fry for a few minutes. Add the zucchini and *soffriggere* or lightly fry the zucchini until still crisp and verdant green. In another pre-heated pan, add a few tablespoons of olive oil and the bread crumbs and sauté the bread crumbs until they are slightly browned. Add the water and bouillon to the zucchini, cooking an additional few minutes until the bouillon dissolves. Add the browned bread crumbs to the zucchini. Combine the drained *al dente* pasta with the saucepan ingredients. Transfer the pasta to a large serving bowl. Top with *pecorino* or *parmigiano* cheese and a little parsley for garnish.

variations: 1) use 2 tablespoons of dried basil or 1/3 cup of torn basil. Fry the disks until golden brown in hot olive oil. Drain on paper towels. Follow the same procedure above adding the sautéed bread crumbs. 2) prepare the zucchini in a batter as in the eggplant recipe on the preceding page.

Spaghetti con gli Zucchini e Funghi- Green summer squash or zucchini with mushrooms is a marriage made in heaven.

Preparation Time: 30 minutes

Ingredients:

- 1 pound of Spaghetti
- 1/2 pound or 4 medium sized zucchini, cubed
- 1 carton of white button mushrooms, sliced
- 4 tablespoons of olive oil
- 1/4 cup of fresh Italian flat-leaf parsley, chopped
- 1 small sweet onion, diced
- 2 whole garlic cloves, minced
- 1/2 cup of dry white wine or water
- 1 Knorr®'s chicken or vegetable bouillon cube

Fill a 10-quart saucepan with water over high heat for the pasta. Add the pasta after the water reaches a boil, approximately 10 minutes before the final preparation of the recipe. Wash and scrub the zucchini and trim off the stem end. Slice the zucchini into 1/5-inch disks then halve into half-moon shapes. Pre-heat a saucepan over medium heat adding the olive oil when hot. Add the garlic, onion, parsley, sliced zucchini and mushrooms, sautéing until the zucchini are still crisp and slightly browned. Add the water or wine and crushed bouillon simmering for another 3 minutes. Combine the drained *al dente* pasta with the zucchini in the saucepan. Toss/mix the ingredients and transfer the completed dish to a large serving bowl. Top with *parmigiano* cheese and a little parsley for garnish.

variations: 1) use 2 tablespoons of dried basil or 1/3 cup of torn basil. 2) prepare the zucchini in a batter as in the eggplant recipe on the preceding page.

Linguine con gli Zucchini e Pomodori- Green summer squash or zucchini with chopped tomatoes.

Preparation Time: 30 minutes

Ingredients:

- 1 pound of Linguine, Spaghetti or Penne
- 1/2 pound or 4 medium sized zucchini, sliced
- 1 (28) ounce or 1 pound 12 ounce can of whole Italian plum tomatoes, diced
- 4 tablespoons of olive oil
- 1/4 cup of fresh Italian flat-leaf parsley, chopped
- 1 small sweet onion, diced
- 2 whole garlic cloves, minced
- 1 Knorr®'s vegetable bouillon cube

Fill a 10-quart saucepan with water over high heat for the pasta. Add the pasta after the water reaches a boil, approximately 10 minutes before the final preparation of the recipe. Wash and scrub the zucchini and trim off the stem end. Slice the zucchini into 1/5-inch disks and cut into half-moons. Pre-heat a saucepan over medium heat adding the olive oil when hot. Add the garlic, onion and the sliced zucchini sautéing the zucchini until still crisp and slightly browned. Add the chopped tomatoes, bouillon and parsley and simmer for 10 minutes. Combine the drained *al dente* pasta with the zucchini and tomatoes in the saucepan. Toss/mix the saucepan ingredients. Transfer the completed dish to a large serving bowl. Top with *parmigiano* cheese and a little parsley for garnish.

variations: 1) use 2 tablespoons of dried basil or 1/4 cup of torn basil. Add mushrooms to the dish when adding the tomatoes. 2) place the completed dish in a flameproof casserole dish. Top with *provolone* or other white-cheese (American Monterey Jack). Place the dish or individual servings under the broiler until the cheese is bubbling and slightly browned in spots.

Linguine con gli Zucchini e Finocchio- Green summer squash or zucchini with chopped fennel.

Preparation Time: 30 minutes

Ingredients:

- 1 pound of Linguine or Penne
- 1/2 pound or 4 medium sized zucchini, cubed
- 1 (28) ounce or 1 pound 12 ounce can of whole Italian plum tomatoes, diced
- 1 small fennel bulb, diced (discard stem and frond)
- 4 tablespoons of olive oil
- 1/4 cup of fresh Italian flat-leaf parsley, chopped
- 2 whole garlic cloves, minced
- 1 Knorr®'s vegetable bouillon cube

Fill a 10-quart saucepan with water over high heat for the pasta. Add the pasta after the water reaches a boil, approximately 10 minutes before the final preparation of the recipe. Wash and scrub the zucchini and trim off the stem end. Slice the zucchini and cut into cubes. Pre-heat a saucepan over medium heat adding the olive oil when hot. Add the garlic and fennel and sauté for a few minutes. Add the sliced zucchini sautéing until the zucchini are still crisp and slightly browned. Add the chopped tomatoes, crushed bouillon and parsley and simmer for 10 minutes. Combine the drained *al dente* pasta with the zucchini and tomatoes in the saucepan. Transfer the completed dish to a large serving bowl. Top with grated *pecorino* cheese and a little parsley for garnish.

variation: use 2 tablespoons of dried basil or 1/3 cup of torn basil. Add mushrooms to the dish when adding the tomatoes.

Ziti di Lusso- Zucchini, tomatoes and mushrooms covered in cheese make this dish a vegetarian's delight. You can do this dish with or without the melted cheese on top.

Preparation Time: 30 minutes

Ingredients:

- 1 pound of Ziti or other tubular pasta
- 1/2 pound or 4 medium sized zucchini, sliced
- 1 (28) ounce or 1 pound 12 ounce can of whole Italian plum tomatoes, diced
- 1 carton of white button mushrooms, sliced
- 4 tablespoons of olive oil
- 1/4 cup of fresh Italian flat-leaf parsley, chopped
- 2 whole garlic cloves, minced
- 1 Knorr®'s chicken bouillon cube
- *provolone* or *mozzarella* cheese, 6 slices (optional)

Fill a 10-quart saucepan with water over high heat for the pasta. Add the pasta after the water reaches a boil, approximately 10 minutes before the final preparation of the recipe. Wash and scrub the zucchini and trim off the stem end. Slice the zucchini into 1/5-inch disks and cut in half-moons. Pre-heat a saucepan over medium heat adding the olive oil when hot. Add the garlic and bouillon and sauté for a few minutes. Add the sliced zucchini and mushrooms, sautéing until the zucchini are still crisp but slightly browned. Add the chopped tomatoes and parsley and simmer for 10 minutes. Combine the drained *al dente* pasta with the zucchini, mushrooms and tomatoes in the saucepan. Toss/mix all of the ingredients. Transfer the completed dish to a large serving bowl. Place *provolone* or other white cheese on top of the pasta and melt the cheese under a broiler. Top with *parmigiano* cheese and a little parsley for garnish.

variation: use 1 tablespoon of dried basil or 1/3 cup torn basil.

Gemelli con gli Asparagi- *Gemelli or* "twins" are the hard little twists more compact than Rotini. Cooked "*al dente*" they are fabulous with a little sauce and vegetables. In this recipe use fresh asparagus tips that you steam in your vegetable steamer. To prepare the asparagus rinse and trim the woody stalks. Steam about 12-15 minutes.

Preparation Time: 30 minutes

Ingredients:

- 1 pound of Gemelli or Rotini
- 1 large fresh bundle of asparagus tips
- 2 ounces of dried *porcini* mushrooms soaked in warm water
- 2 cups of white button mushrooms, sliced
- 1 (28) ounce or 1 pound 12 ounce can of crushed tomatoes
- 4 tablespoons of olive oil
- 1/4 cup of fresh Italian flat-leaf parsley, chopped
- 4 whole garlic cloves, minced
- 1 Knorr®'s vegetable bouillon cube
- 1/2 cup of dry white wine or water

Fill a 10-quart saucepan with water over high heat for the pasta. Add the pasta after the water reaches a boil, approximately 10 minutes before the final preparation of the recipe. Place the dried *porcini* mushrooms in a small bowl and barely cover with lukewarm water for 10 minutes. Take the asparagus, cut in half and use only the tips. Place the asparagus tips in the steamer and steam for 12 minutes. Steam until still crisp and verdant green in color. Pre-heat a saucepan over high heat, adding the olive oil when hot. Sauté the garlic, white button mushrooms, *porcini* with liquid, and the parsley for a few minutes. Add the white wine and crushed bouillon cube to saucepan and simmer for a few minutes until the bouillon is dissolved. Add the tomatoes to the saucepan and simmer with the other ingredients for 10 minutes. Meanwhile cook the pasta. When the asparagus is ready add it to the saucepan. Continue simmering the tomato/asparagus mixture for a few minutes. Combine the *al dente* pasta with the saucepan ingredients and cook for an additional minute. Transfer the completed dish to a large serving bowl and top with grated *pecorino* cheese and any remaining parsley.

variation: Add hot pepper flakes for an "*arrabbiata*" zing. Substitute sage for parsley.

Wide angle view of my Grandfather's *Trullo* house, birthplace and farm in the countryside of Cisternino. Across from the house lies *Monte Pagano* where the Greeks fought the Romans in a battle sometime in the 3rd century BC.

Tortellini alla Cremona- Everyone is familiar with *Tortellini* stuffed with cheese, meat, or pumpkin, and almost as many folks know of the legend that *Tortellini* were inspired by the navel of Venus of times past. The first time I tried this Northern Italian dish was in 1976 in a *tratorria* off of the Academia Bridge. *"Ai Cugnaï"* was a popular student-eating establishment because of the reasonable prices and *"casalinga"* or home-cooked meals. It was there when we were awaiting our food I asked Etta our hostess what the young man at an adjacent table was being served. No sooner said that the stranger offered me a taste. Being a fearless and hungry student I couldn't refuse and I became as enamored of the *Tortellini* as many of my fellow countrymen are today. *Tortellini* is best in a cream or tomato/cream sauce or my *besciamella* sauce on page 22. This recipe reminds me of the modern Northern Italian cuisine one might find in Cremona.

Preparation Time: 30 minutes

Ingredients:

- 1 pound of cheese filled Tortellini
- 2 ounces of dried *porcini* mushrooms (strictly optional)
- 1 cup of button, brown *cremini* or *portabella* mushrooms, sliced
- 1 cup of sun dried tomatoes
- 1 large roasted red pepper from a jar, sliced or a fresh red pepper roasted under the broiler, cooled and skinned.
- 4 tablespoons of olive oil
- 1 whole garlic clove, minced
- ½ of a Knorr®'s chicken bouillon or *porcini* mushroom bouillon cube
- 2 pints of heavy cream

Fill a 10-quart saucepan with water over high heat for the pasta. Add the pasta after the water reaches a boil, approximately 10 minutes before the final preparation of the recipe. Place the dried *porcini* mushrooms in a small bowl and barely cover with lukewarm water for 10 minutes. Halve the roasted red pepper from the jar. Clean and then dice mushrooms. Pre-heat a saucepan over medium heat, adding the olive oil when hot. **Soffriggere** or lightly fry the garlic, the mushrooms (and *porcini* with liquid), sliced or julienne red pepper and the parsley in the olive oil for a few minutes. Add the bouillon cube, the sun-dried tomatoes and a little water or dry white wine and cook an additional 10 minutes. Finally add the heavy cream and heat through until hot and bubbly. If the sauce isn't thick enough, mix 1 tablespoon of cornstarch with ½ cup of water, stir and add to the sauce. Combine the *al dente* pasta with the saucepan ingredients. Transfer the completed dish to a large serving bowl. Serve with grated *parmigiano* cheese apart.

variation: cut the cream with one cup of *pomodoro* sauce to make a "pink" or *rosa* sauce.

Spaghetti Milanese- Among the most recent new cuisine dishes this one has been one of the more successful attempts at introducing an ingredient that albeit common in the kitchen is not associated with pasta sauces. The Worcestershire sauce is used here as a substitute for veal stock.

Preparation Time: 30 minutes

Ingredients:

- 1 pound of Spaghetti
- small package of dried *porcini* mushrooms (strictly optional)
- 1/2 pound of fresh mushrooms, any type: button, brown *cremini* or *portabella* mushrooms, sliced
- 1 (28 ounce) or 1 pound 12 ounce can of whole tomatoes, drained and diced
- a pinch of oregano
- 1/4 cup of fresh Italian flat-leaf parsley, chopped
- 2 tablespoons of olive oil
- 2 whole garlic cloves, minced
- 2 anchovy fillets or a teaspoon of anchovy paste
- 1 Knorr®'s chicken bouillon cube
- 2 tablespoons of Worcestershire sauce

Fill a 10-quart saucepan with water over high heat for the pasta. Add the pasta after the water reaches a boil, approximately 10 minutes before the final preparation of the recipe. Place the dried *porcini* mushrooms in a small bowl and barely cover with lukewarm water for 10 minutes. Pre-heat a saucepan over medium heat, adding the olive oil when hot. *Soffriggere* or lightly fry the garlic, parsley, mushrooms (and *porcini* with liquid), oregano and two anchovy fillets or a little anchovy paste for 5 minutes or until the anchovy fillets dissolve. Add the crushed bouillon cube, a little water or dry white wine and the tomatoes. Simmer all of the ingredients for 15 minutes, adding the Worcestershire sauce the last 5 minutes of cooking. Combine the *al dente* pasta with the saucepan ingredients. Transfer the pasta to a large serving bowl. Garnish with parsley. Serve with grated *parmigiano* cheese apart.

Orecchiette con 'Rucola ("little ears" with arugula greens)- This a traditional vegetable dish from my region of Apulia that is rich in fresh vegetables. If you can't find *orecchiette* in the supermarket, little shells, spirals or butterfly pasta will do just fine.

Preparation Time: 25 minutes

Ingredients:

- 1 pound of Orecchiette or Spaghetti
- 1 pound of mixed greens: arugula, Swiss chard, chicory or escarole, fresh spinach with stems removed, or substitute with 1 large can of "Glory" brand mixed greens
- 1/2 of a head of cauliflower, chopped
- 1/4 cup of fresh Italian flat-leaf parsley, chopped
- 4 tablespoons of olive oil
- 2 whole garlic cloves, minced
- 1/2 of a Knorr®'s vegetable bouillon cube
- 1/2 cup of water
- salt and pepper to taste

Fill a 10-quart saucepan with water over high heat for the pasta. Add the pasta and the chopped greens to the boiling pot of water for 8-10 minutes. Chop the cauliflower and place in a steamer for 10 minutes or steam in the bottom of a pot with water lining the bottom. Drain the cooked pasta and greens. In a pre-heated saucepan, sauté the cauliflower with the half-bouillon cube, water, olive oil, garlic and parsley for 5 minutes. Take care not to burn the cauliflower but having a little brown edge on the cauliflower is good. Add the cooked, drained greens and *al dente* pasta to the saucepan with the sautéed cauliflower. Drizzle a little extra-virgin olive oil on top and mix well. Season with salt and pepper. Transfer the completed dish to a large serving bowl. Top with grated *pecorino* cheese. Garnish with parsley.

Orecchiette con Cime di Rapa ("little ears" with turnip greens)- This is a vegetable dish from my region of Apulia that has a traditional cuisine rich in fresh vegetables. If you can't find *orecchiette* in the supermarket, little shells, spirals or butterfly pasta will be just fine.

Preparation Time: 25 minutes

Ingredients:

- 1 pound of Orecchiette
- 2 pounds of turnip greens (use only the most tender leaves) or substitute with a can of "Glory" brand cooked Turnip Greens
- 4 anchovy fillets packed in oil with capers
- 4 tablespoons of olive oil
- 2 whole garlic cloves, minced
- a pinch of red pepper flakes
- 1/2 of a Knorr®'s vegetable bouillon cube
- 1/4 cup of fresh Italian flat-leaf parsley, chopped

Fill a 10-quart saucepan with water over high heat for the pasta. Add the pasta after the water reaches a boil, approximately 10 minutes before the final preparation of the recipe. In a pre-heated saucepan, *soffriggere* or lightly fry sauté the anchovies, bouillon cube, capers, garlic parsley, and red pepper flakes in the olive oil for 5 minutes or until the anchovies dissolve. Add the raw greens and 1/2 cup of water to the saucepan simmering all ingredients for 15 minutes. Add a little pasta water to the saucepan if the ingredients become too dry. Add the drained *al dente* pasta to the saucepan and mix well. Drizzle a little extra-virgin olive oil on top. Season with salt and pepper. Transfer the completed dish to a large serving bowl. Top with grated *pecorino* cheese.

Orecchiette Arrabbiata ("angry little ears")- The spicy red chill peppers are widely used in *Puglia*. If you can't find *orecchiette* in the supermarket, little shells, spirals or butterfly pasta will be just fine.

Preparation Time: 20 minutes

Ingredients:

- 1 pound of Orecchiette
- 15 cherry tomatoes, halved
- 4 anchovy fillets packed in oil
- 1/4 cup of fresh Italian flat-leaf parsley, chopped
- 1 tablespoon of capers
- a pinch of red pepper flakes
- 2 tablespoons of pitted black olives
- 4 tablespoons of olive oil
- 2 whole garlic cloves, minced

Fill a 10-quart saucepan with water over high heat for the pasta. Add the pasta after the water reaches a boil. In a pre-heated saucepan, *soffriggere* or lightly fry the garlic, anchovies, tomatoes, olives, capers, parsley and red pepper flakes in the olive oil for 5-8 minutes. Combine and toss the drained *al dente* pasta with the saucepan ingredients. Transfer the completed dish to a large serving bowl. Top with grated *pecorino* cheese. Garnish with parsley.

Rigatoni con Ricotta e Zucchini- Pasta with ricotta cheese and zucchini or green squash.

Preparation Time: 30 minutes

Ingredients:

- 1 pound of Rigatoni
- 8 ounces of ricotta cheese
- 4 small zucchini or green squash, sliced
- 1 (28 ounce) or 1 pound 12 ounce can of whole plum tomatoes, drained and diced
- 4 tablespoons of olive oil
- 1/4 cup of fresh basil, shredded or torn
- 2 whole garlic cloves, minced
- 1 small sweet onion, diced
- ½ of a Knorr®'s vegetable bouillon cube

Fill a 10-quart saucepan with water over high heat for the pasta. Add the pasta after the water reaches a boil, approximately 10 minutes before the final preparation of the recipe. Prepare the zucchini by washing and paring off the ends. Slice the zucchini into 1/5-inch disks. *Soffriggere* or lightly fry the garlic, onions and zucchini in a pre-heated saucepan with olive oil for a few minutes. Add the tomatoes, basil, and bouillon and simmer for 10 minutes. Drain the *al dente* pasta and toss with the ricotta cheese. Combine and toss the pasta with the saucepan ingredients. Transfer the completed dish to a large serving bowl. Serve with *parmigiano* cheese apart.

Penne Caponata Angelo (eggplant, peppers, capers)- Known as a relish from the mountainous Abruzzo region and a dish which reminds me of my beloved landlord's family, the Pelusi's, when we lived in Thiene, Italy. Angelo Pelusi is Abruzzese, and like many of his fellow countrymen, prefers food hot and spicy.

Preparation Time: 30 minutes

Ingredients:

- 1 pound of Penne
- 1 pound of eggplant, sliced and cubed
- 1 (28) ounce or 1 pound 12 ounce can of crushed tomatoes
- 1/2 of a green pepper and 1/2 of a red pepper, sliced
- 2 tablespoons of capers
- 5 tablespoons of olive oil or as needed (qb) quanto basta
- 1/4 cup of fresh basil, shredded or torn
- 2 whole garlic cloves, minced
- 1 small sweet onion, diced
- 1 tablespoon of Balsamic vinegar
- 1 Knorr®'s vegetable bouillon cube
- a pinch of hot pepper flakes

Fill a 10-quart saucepan with water over high heat for the pasta. Add the pasta after the water reaches a boil, approximately 10 minutes before the final preparation of the recipe. Prepare the eggplant by washing and paring off the ends. Slice the eggplant and cut into 1-inch cubes. Halve the peppers, de-rib, de-seed and then slice the peppers into long, thin slices. In a pre-heated saucepan, with 2 tablespoons of olive oil, *soffriggere* or lightly fry the garlic and onion for a few minutes. Add the other 3 tablespoons of olive oil and fry the eggplant and peppers for about 5 minutes until the eggplant are slightly browned and the peppers supple. You can broil the peppers per previous recipes if desired or use roasted peppers from a jar. Add the tomatoes, capers, basil, balsamic vinegar, hot pepper flakes and bouillon to the saucepan. Simmer for 15 minutes. Combine and toss the *al dente* pasta with the saucepan ingredients. Transfer the completed dish to a large serving bowl. Serve with grated *pecorino* or *parmigiano* cheese apart.

Rotini con i Carciofi e Cannellini (corkscrew pasta with artichoke hearts and white kidney beans)- Apulia is renown for its wonderful artichokes. On my first visit to Cisternino, my cousin Querico's wife prepared the best-fried artichokes I have ever tasted.

Preparation Time: 30 minutes

Ingredients:

* 1 pound of Rotini
* 1 (12 ounce) can of artichoke hearts in water or oil, drained and chopped
* 1 can of *cannellini* (white kidney beans), drained
* 1/4 each red, yellow, and green pepper, sliced or substitute with red pepper
* 4 ounces of fresh baby spinach leaves
* 5 tablespoon of olive oil or as needed (qb) quanto basta in Italian
* 1/4 cup of fresh Italian flat-leaf parsley, chopped
* 2 whole garlic cloves, minced
* 1 small sweet onion, diced
* 1/2 of a Knorr®'s vegetable bouillon cube

Fill a 10-quart saucepan with water over high heat for the pasta. Add the pasta after the water reaches a boil, approximately 10 minutes before the final preparation of the recipe. Prepare the peppers by halving, de-ribbing and de-seeding. Place the peppers under a broiler skin side up until the skin is charred black. Remove from heat, run under cold water, peeling off skin. Slice the peppers into strips and place on a plate. Cover with a few drops of olive oil. Chop the artichokes into small pieces. In a pre-heated saucepan, with 2 tablespoons of olive oil, *soffriggere* or lightly fry the garlic and onion for a few minutes. Add the artichokes, peppers, spinach, bouillon cube, parsley and the other 3 tablespoons of olive oil and fry for about 3 minutes. Add the beans, and continue simmering for 5 minutes. Drain the *al dente* pasta and toss with the saucepan ingredients. Transfer the completed dish to a large serving bowl. Serve with grated *pecorino* or *parmigiano* cheese apart.

variation: make it *arrabbiata* with hot pepper flakes.

Rigatoni Pugliese- This recipe with its combination of eggplant, capers and artichokes is typical of my Grandparent's region in the "Heel of the Boot". Artichokes are a major crop in this sun-laden zone.

Preparation Time: 30 minutes

Ingredients:

- 1 pound of Rigatoni
- 1 medium-sized eggplant, cubed
- 2 -3 zucchini, cubed
- 1 (12) ounce can or jar of artichoke hearts in water or oil, drained and chopped
- 1/2 can of *cannellini* (white kidney beans) drained
- 1 each red, yellow, and green pepper, sliced or substitute with commercial red peppers from a jar
- 2 tablespoons of capers
- 1/4 cup of pitted black olives, chopped
- 6 tablespoons of olive oil or as needed (qb) quanto basta in Italian
- 1/4 cup of fresh Italian flat-leaf parsley, chopped
- 1 tablespoon of tomato paste
- 2 whole garlic cloves, minced
- 1 small sweet onion, chopped
- 1/2 of a Knorr®'s vegetable bouillon cube

Fill a 10-quart saucepan with water over high heat for the pasta. Add the pasta after the water reaches a boil, approximately 10 minutes before the final preparation of the recipe. Prepare the peppers by halving, de-ribbing and de-seeding. Place the peppers under a broiler skin side up until the skin is charred black. Remove from heat, run under cold water, peeling off skin. Slice the peppers into strips and place on a plate. Drizzle the peppers with a few drops of olive oil. Chop the artichokes into small pieces. Chop the eggplant and zucchini into cubes. *Soffriggere* or lightly fry the garlic and onions in a heated saucepan with 2 tablespoons of olive oil for a few minutes. Add the artichokes, peppers, eggplant, zucchini, capers, olives, parsley, bouillon cube, tomato paste, 1/4 cup water and the other 4 tablespoons of olive oil and simmer for about 15 minutes. Add the beans to the saucepan and simmer for 5 minutes. Drain the *al dente* pasta and toss with the saucepan ingredients. Transfer the completed dish to a large serving bowl. Serve with grated *pecorino* cheese apart.

Rotini con le Melanzane e Zucchini- Spiral pasta with eggplant and zucchini "Apulian Style".

Preparation Time: 30 minutes

Ingredients:

- 1 pound of Rotini
- 1 small-sized eggplant, cubed
- 2 zucchini, peeled and cubed
- 1 (28) ounce or 1 pound 12 ounce can of whole plum tomatoes, diced
- 4 tablespoons of olive oil or as needed (qb) quanto basta in Italian
- 1/4 cup of fresh Italian flat-leaf parsley, chopped
- 1 small sweet onion, chopped
- 4 whole garlic cloves, minced
- 1 Knorr®'s vegetable bouillon cube
- salt and pepper to taste

Fill a 10-quart saucepan with water over high heat for the pasta. Add the pasta after the water reaches a boil, approximately 10 minutes before the final preparation of the recipe. In a pre-heated saucepan, sauté the garlic, onion, cubed eggplant and zucchini with 4 tablespoons of olive oil for a few minutes. Add the diced tomatoes with liquid, parsley and bouillon cube and simmer for about 15 minutes. Drain the *al dente* pasta and toss with the saucepan ingredients. Transfer the completed dish to a large serving bowl. Serve with grated *parmigiano* and *pecorino* cheese apart as well.

variation: make the dish *"arrabbiata"* by adding hot pepper flakes.

Ziti Tri-Colore (three colored)-This dish evokes the colors of the Italian flag (green, white, red) like a pizza Margherita by combining spinach, white *cannellini* beans, and tomatoes.

Preparation Time: 30 minutes

Ingredients:

- 1 pound of Ziti or other tubular pasta
- 1 bag of fresh spinach, chopped or 1 box of frozen chopped spinach
- 1/2 can of *cannellini* beans, drained of liquid
- 1 (28) ounce) or 1 pound 12 ounce can of whole tomatoes, chopped.
- 4 tablespoons of olive oil
- 1/4 cup of fresh basil, shredded or torn
- 2 whole garlic cloves, minced
- 1 Knorr®'s vegetable bouillon cube
- salt and pepper to taste

Fill a 10-quart saucepan with water over high heat for the pasta. Add the pasta after the water reaches a boil, approximately 10 minutes before the final preparation of the recipe. Prepare the fresh spinach by washing, draining and chopping. In a pre-heated saucepan, with two tablespoons of olive oil, ***soffriggere*** or lightly fry the garlic for a few minutes. Add frozen or freshly chopped spinach to the saucepan and the other two tablespoons of olive oil. Fry the spinach for about 5 minutes. Add the tomatoes, beans, basil, and bouillon to the saucepan with the spinach. Simmer for 15 minutes. Combine the drained *al dente* pasta with the saucepan ingredients. Top with a few tablespoons of *pecorino* cheese. Transfer the completed dish to a large serving bowl. Serve with grated *parmigiano* and or *pecorino* cheese apart as well.

Tagliatelle con Ceci e Fave- This Apulian dish combines two of the local legumes served with pasta as my relatives in Cisternino prepare it. Within the whitewashed town walls, once an Aragonese Spanish fortress, or out in the countryside cone-shaped *Trulli* houses, the wonderful aroma of *ceci* and *fave* beans fill the air, especially at the noon's meal. Once considered peasant fare, people everywhere are rediscovering the healthfulness and flavor in bean and pasta dishes.

Preparation Time: 30 minutes

Ingredients:

- 1 pound of Tagliatelle or other ribbon pasta (tubular pasta works well also)
- 1 can of *ceci* or garbanzo beans, drained
- 1 can of *fava* beans, drained (found in Italian deli's or specialty food shops)
- 2 tablespoons of tomato paste
- 1 tablespoon of dried rosemary
- 1/2 of a celery stalk, minced
- 4 tablespoons of olive oil or as needed (qb) quanto basta in Italian
- 2 whole garlic cloves, minced
- 1/2 of a Knorr®'s vegetable bouillon cube
- salt and pepper to taste

Fill a 10-quart saucepan with water over high heat for the pasta. Add the pasta after the water reaches a boil, approximately 10 minutes before the final preparation of the recipe. Prepare the *ceci* and *fava* beans by pureeing them in a food processor with 2 tablespoons or qb of olive oil until the beans become a thick paste. In a pre-heated saucepan with 2 tablespoons olive oil, *soffriggere* or lightly fry the garlic, minced celery, bouillon and rosemary for a few minutes. Add the creamed beans and the tomato paste to the saucepan pan with the already cooked garlic (which can be discarded with the rosemary). Simmer this mixture until hot and bubbly. Add a little pasta water if the dish seems too dry. Combine the drained *al dente* pasta with the bean puree in the saucepan along with a few tablespoons of *pecorino* cheese. Transfer the completed dish to a large serving bowl. Serve with grated *parmigiano* and or *pecorino* cheese apart as well.

Ziti con Tre Fagioli- Three beans: fresh green beans, *ceci* beans, and *cannellini* comprise this flavorful *pasta & fagioli piatto*.

Preparation Time: 30 minutes

Ingredients:

- 1 pound of Ziti
- 1/2 can of *ceci* or garbanzo beans, drained
- 1/2 can of *cannellini* beans, drained
- 1/2 pound of fresh green beans
- 1 (14.5) ounce can of diced tomatoes
- 1/4 cup of fresh Italian flat-leaf parsley, chopped
- 4 tablespoons of olive oil
- 2 whole garlic cloves, minced
- 1 Knorr®'s vegetable bouillon cube

Fill a 10-quart saucepan with water over high heat for the pasta. Add the pasta during the last 10 minutes of the preparation process to the boiling water. Steam the fresh green beans until cooked but still crisp in a vegetable steamer (10 minutes) or add the beans to the next step with the tomatoes. In a pre-heated saucepan, with 2 tablespoons of olive oil, *soffriggere* or lightly fry the garlic for a few minutes. Add the diced tomatoes, bouillon, and parsley and simmer for 10 minutes. Add all of the beans and simmer for an additional 5 minutes. Combine the drained *al dente* pasta with the beans in the saucepan. Toss the ingredients. Add a few tablespoons of *pecorino* cheese. Transfer the completed dish to a large serving bowl. Serve with grated *parmigiano* and or *pecorino* cheese apart as well.

Penne con Broccoli e Fagioli (red or white kidney beans)- Broccoli and red kidney or *cannellini* beans comprise this flavorful *pasta & fagioli piatto.*

Preparation Time: 30 minutes

Ingredients:

- 1 pound of Penne noodles
- 1 can of *cannellini* beans or red kidney beans, drained
- 1 head of broccoli, pared into florets
- 1 (14.5) ounce can of diced tomatoes
- 1/4 cup of fresh Italian flat-leaf parsley, chopped
- 4 tablespoons of olive oil
- 2 whole garlic cloves, minced
- 1 Knorr®'s vegetable bouillon cube

Fill a 10-quart saucepan with water over high heat for the pasta. Add the pasta during the last 10 minutes of the preparation process to the boiling water. Steam the fresh broccoli until cooked but still crisp in a vegetable steamer (10 minutes). You can pare the broccoli into little florets before or after steaming. In a pre-heated saucepan, with 2 tablespoons of olive oil, *soffriggere* or lightly fry the garlic for a few minutes. Add the diced tomatoes, bouillon, and parsley and simmer for 5 minutes. Add all of the chopped broccoli and beans to the saucepan and simmer for an additional 5 minutes. Combine the drained *al dente* pasta with the beans in the saucepan. Add a few tablespoons of *pecorino* cheese. Transfer the completed dish to a large serving bowl. Serve with grated *parmigiano* and or *pecorino* cheese apart as well

variation: make the dish *"arrabbiata"* by adding hot pepper flakes.

Spaghetti con Funghi e Melanzane (mushrooms and eggplant)

Preparation Time: 30 minutes

Ingredients:

- 1 pound of Spaghetti
- 1 medium-sized eggplant, cubed (if possible pre-soaked in salted water under a weight then cubed, squeezed of moisture and patted dry prior to cooking))
- 1/2 pound of fresh white button, brown *cremini* or *portabella* mushrooms
- 4 ounces of dried *porcini* mushrooms covered in water (optional)
- 1/2 cup of fresh Italian flat-leaf parsley, chopped
- 4 tablespoons of olive oil or as needed (qb) quanto basta as needed
- 2 whole garlic cloves, minced
- 1 Knorr®'s chicken bouillon cube or *porcini* mushroom bouillon cube if available
- 1/2 cup of water
- salt and pepper to taste

Fill a 10-quart saucepan with water over high heat for the pasta. Add the pasta after the water reaches a boil, approximately 10 minutes before the final preparation of the recipe. Pre-heat a saucepan with the olive oil. Add the garlic, cubed eggplant, the sliced mushrooms, and the parsley, and sauté for 5 minutes. After 5 minutes or so, add the bouillon cube along with 1/2 cup of water (and the optional *porcini* mushrooms in water). Simmer all ingredients for an additional 10 minutes. Combine the drained *al dente* pasta with the eggplant /mushroom mixture in the saucepan. Add a few tablespoons of *parmigiano* cheese. Transfer the completed dish to a large serving bowl. Serve with grated *parmigiano* and *pecorino* cheese apart as well.

variation: make the dish *"arrabbiata"* by adding hot pepper flakes.

Spaghetti con Cavolfiore (cauliflower)- This dish uses a flavorful *dolce-amaro* sweet-sour tomato sauce that is typical of southern Italy and Apulia.

Preparation Time: 30 minutes

Ingredients:

- 1 pound of Spaghetti
- 1 large head of cauliflower, cut into florets
- 1/4 cup of black *gaeta* olives or other black olive, pitted and chopped
- 2 anchovy fillets or 1 teaspoon of anchovy paste
- 1 (28) ounce or 1 pound 12 ounce can of crushed tomatoes
- 1 tablespoon of balsamic vinegar
- 1 teaspoon of sugar
- 1/2 cup of fresh Italian flat-leaf parsley, chopped
- 4 tablespoons of olive oil
- 2 whole garlic cloves, minced
- 1 Knorr®'s chicken bouillon cube
- salt and white pepper to taste

Fill a 10-quart saucepan with water over high heat for the pasta. Add the pasta after the water reaches a boil, approximately 10 minutes before the final preparation of the recipe. Pre-heat a saucepan with the olive oil. *Soffriggere* or lightly fry the garlic in a heated saucepan, with 4 tablespoons of olive oil for a few minutes. Add the cauliflower florets and cook until slightly browned on both sides. Add the parsley, olives, tomatoes, anchovy paste and bouillon and simmer an additional 10 minutes. In a bowl combine the balsamic vinegar and sugar. Add the vinegar /sugar (*dolce-amaro*) mixture to the cauliflower and tomato sauce. Simmer all of the ingredients for an additional 5 minutes. Combine the drained *al dente* pasta with the cauliflower mixture in the saucepan. Add a few tablespoons of *parmigiano* cheese. Transfer the completed dish to a large serving bowl. Serve with grated *parmigiano* or *pecorino* cheese apart as well.

Spaghetti al Pesto- I had to include some sort of Ligurian style pesto sauce because of its popularity. In a pesto that comes from using the pestle and mortar to grind the basil, you can also substitute parsley or other herbs and keep it in your refrigerator to top fish or meat dishes. Also called a *sugo verde* or green sauce.

Preparation Time: 30 minutes

Ingredients:

- 1 pound of Spaghetti
- 20-25 fresh basil leaves
- 2 tablespoons of *pinoli* or pine nuts, toasted in a pan
- 1 cup of olive oil
- 4 whole garlic cloves, minced
- salt and pepper to taste

Fill a 10-quart saucepan with water over high heat for the pasta. Add the pasta after the water reaches a boil, approximately 10 minutes before the final preparation of the recipe. In a food processor, place garlic, olive oil and toasted pine nuts or *pinoli*. Use the metal blade and grind until fine. Combine the drained *al dente* pasta with the pesto mixture in the 10-quart saucepan. Add a few tablespoons of *parmigiano* cheese. Toss the ingredients. Transfer the completed dish to a large serving bowl. Serve with grated *parmigiano* cheese apart as well

variations: 1) add a pound of blanched chopped tomatoes to the food processor with the pesto. Blanch tomatoes by placing them in boiling water for a minute. Cool, remove skin and seeds and chop up for addition to the pesto sauce. 2) use parsley in place of basil or 3) use basil and parsley together.

Amphoras are still used today to store wine and produce. Inside the *Trullo* house, wine is stored underneath the kitchen floor. My cousin lifted a large flagstone tile to reveal two huge vats of white and red wine. Giovanni was adamant in saying his wine was made without chemicals. The white wine was cool, dry and had a slight blush to it. The local white wine is called *Locorotondo* after a neighboring village and is an outstanding dry white wine. Apulian grapes are shipped world wide and used to "cut" other wines in order to bring them up to fermentation standards. The hearty red grape called *Primitivo* is used in California to produce Zinfandel wine.

A *Trullo* dwelling in Alberobello. Note the Christian cross symbol on the
dome. In Cisternino dialect local inhabitants are referred to as "*Cristiene or
Cristiani*", meaning Christians. This colloquialism came about for two
reasons. First, the Saracens and Ottoman Turks subjected the region to
many brutal raids and invasions so the term "*Cristiene*" was used to
differentiate between the invader and the natives. Secondly, Apulia was the
launching point for the Norman and Venetian Crusades to the Holy Land.
The local dialect in Cisternino has a heavy Norman influence; nouns such as
"sea" pronounced "*Mere*" in *Cistranese* instead of the Italian "*Mare*" are
French in pronunciation rather than Italian.

Meat-based Sauces
I Carni

In this section I will concentrate on pasta dishes that have some type of meat whether it be a smattering of *prosciutto* or sauces made with 1/2 pound or so of ground veal, turkey, chicken, beef or pork. Once again all items can be readily found in most supermarkets and are included in the shopping list so these meals can be made from items I have recommended you stock in your *"cucina Italiana"*. You can substitute the meat with bouillon in some cases but overall meat-based dishes will not be low in fat so enjoy them as the Italians do guilt-free, then take a *"passeggiata"* or long walk!

My Great-Grandmother Scarafile in front of her *Trullo*. *Carne Cortile* or courtyard animals like the sheep and goat in the photo are the main sources for dairy and meat in the region of *Puglia*. Chickens and rabbits are also kept as courtyard game.

Sunday Tagliatelle Bolognese- I placed this dish in the cookbook even though the preparation time parameter conflicts with the theme of *"presto"* preparation. This is the Sunday special meal for the family where extra time is available needed to prepare this sauce. Bologna, the culinary capital of Italy, abounds in heavy cream and meats sauces that we Americans like. In this dish a 2 to 2 &1/2 pound London Broil or Bottom Round Roast or any type of beef roast is cooked in a Dutch oven or crock-pot until the meat can be pulled apart in strips.

Preparation Time: 3 hours

Ingredients:

- 1 to 1 1/2 pounds of Tagliatelle or other ribbon noodle (Fettuccine)
- 2 to 2 1/2 pound beef roast
- 1 carrot, chopped
- 1 celery stalk, chopped
- 1 onion, diced
- 1 teaspoon of dried rosemary
- 1 tablespoon of dried basil
- 4 tablespoons of olive oil
- 1/4 cup of fresh Italian flat-leaf parsley, chopped
- 4 whole garlic cloves, minced
- 1 (28) ounce or 1 pound 12 ounce can of crushed tomatoes
- 4 tablespoons of tomato paste
- 2 Knorr®'s beef bouillon cubes
- 1 pint of heavy cream
- 1 pinch of nutmeg and cinnamon
- 1/2 cup of dry white wine

Fill a 10-quart saucepan with water over medium high heat for the pasta after the meat sauce is completed. Add the olive oil to a Dutch Oven heating on the stovetop until the oil is hot. Add the roast and brown on both sides. Add the chopped onion, garlic, celery and carrot and sauté for a few minutes. Place the Dutch Oven in a oven pre-heated to 350 degrees F° and cook for 2 hours until the meat is tender and pulls apart easily. Remove the roast from the Dutch Oven and hand-pull or cut into pieces. Re-add the beef to the Dutch Oven. Add the tomatoes, bouillon, wine, rosemary, basil, parsley and tomato paste to the Dutch Oven with the pulled beef. Cook in the oven for an additional hour. Finish the sauce by adding the heavy cream, stirring until the cream is incorporated. Add optional nutmeg and cinnamon (pinch). Place the *al dente* tagliatelle or fettuccine in a serving bowl, pour over the sauce and mix well. Top with *parmigiano* cheese. Serve with grated *parmigiano* cheese apart in a bowl as well.

Bucatini alla Matriciana (tubular pasta Matriciana)- This is a classic dish served though out Italy but is a specialty of the mountainous Abruzzi region. The dish is also referred to as *"Amatriciana"* from one of the Sabine villages. One of the most original presentations of this dish I had was in a small *trattoria* in Vicenza and more recently in Campo dei Fiori in Rome. Traditionally "hog jowl"or *guanciale,* which can be found in supermarkets, is used but Italian *pancetta* or regular bacon can be substituted for *guanciale.*

Preparation Time: 30 minutes

Ingredients:

- 1 pound of Bucatini (tubular spaghetti)
- 1/4 pound of *pancetta*, bacon or hog jowl (*guanciale*), cubed
- 1/2 of a medium-sized onion, diced
- 2 cloves of minced garlic
- 1 (28) ounce or 1 pound 12 ounce can of whole San Marzano plum tomatoes, diced
- 1 tablespoon of olive oil
- Torn fresh basil leaves
- hot pepper flakes or diced red *pepperoncini* (qb)
- pecorino grattugiato (grated pecorino is a must)

Fill a 10-quart saucepan with water over high heat for the pasta. Add the pasta during the last 10 minutes of the preparation process to the boiling water. Pre-heat a saucepan with the olive oil. Add the cubed bacon or *pancetta or guanciale* and sauté until the bacon is browned but not crispy (3-4 minutes). Use a slotted spoon to remove the bacon and set aside on a plate. Add the onion and garlic to the same pan and *soffriggere* or lightly fry for a few minutes. Add the cooked bacon, tomatoes, basil, and hot pepper flakes. Simmer an additional 10-15 minutes. Combine the *al dente* pasta with the saucepan ingredients and simmer for a few more minutes. Transfer the completed dish to a large serving bowl. Top with *pecorino* cheese. Serve with grated *pecorino* cheese apart as well.

Rotini Tri-Colore col Prosciutto e Spinaci (spirals in three colors with ham and spinach)- This dish has a *besciamella* or white sauce that is browned under a broiler.

Preparation Time: 30 minutes

Ingredients:

- 1 pound of multi-colored spirals or regular Rotini (red, white, green,)
- 1/4 pound of or *prosciutto crudo* (cured*)* or *prosciutto cotto* (cooked), chopped
- 1 small sweet onion, diced
- 1 bag of fresh spinach, chopped or 1 box of frozen chopped spinach
- 2 cups mushrooms, sliced
- 4 tablespoons of unsalted butter
- 3 tablespoons of flour
- 1 & 1/2 cups of whole milk
- 1 tablespoon of olive oil
- 1/2 of a Knorr®'s chicken bouillon cube
- 1 cup of *parmigiano-reggiano* cheese

Fill a 10-quart saucepan with water over high heat for the pasta. Add the pasta during the last 10 minutes of the preparation process to the boiling water. Pre-heat a saucepan with the olive oil. Add the cubed ham or *prosciutto*, onion, chopped spinach and sliced mushrooms and *soffriggere* or lightly fry for 5 minutes. While that preparation is cooking, heat a saucepan over low heat and add the butter. When the butter melts add the flour and use a wooden spoon to mix the butter and flour. Add the whole milk and bouillon cube and turn up the heat stirring with a whisk until the sauce thickens. (This is the *besciamella* sauce found on page 22.) Place the white sauce pan aside and turn off the pan with the sautéed vegetables and ham as well. When the pasta is cooked *al dente*, drain and place the pasta and spinach-ham mixture in an ovenproof dish. Pour the white sauce on top. Top with the grated *parmigiano* cheese. Place the ovenproof dish or bowl under the broiler until the topping is browned but not burned. Serve in the ovenproof dish on a coaster. Serve with extra grated *parmigiano* cheese apart as well.

Tortellini alla Panna, Prosciutto e Piselli-*Tortellini* pasta in a cream sauce with ham and peas.

Preparation Time: 40 minutes

Ingredients:

- 1 pound of fresh cheese-filled Tortellini or dried variety of the same
- 1/4 pound of or *prosciutto crudo* (cured) or *prosciutto cotto* (cooked) or substitute Canadian bacon, cubed
- 1 small sweet onion, diced
- 2 whole garlic cloves, minced
- 1 cup of frozen peas
- 4 tablespoons of unsalted butter
- 2 pints or 1 quart of heavy cream or substitute with *besciamella* sauce (see recipe on page 22)
- 1 Knorr®'s chicken bouillon cube
- 1 cup of *parmigiano-reggiano* cheese
- one pinch of nutmeg and cinnamon

Fill a 10-quart saucepan with water over high heat for the pasta. Add the pasta and frozen peas during the last 10 minutes of the preparation process to the boiling water. Pre-heat a saucepan with the olive oil. Add the cubed ham or *prosciutto*, onion and garlic and ***soffriggere*** or lightly fry for 5 minutes. Add the heavy cream and bouillon cube to the sautéed ingredients. Break up the bouillon cube with a wooden spoon so it dissolves in the heavy cream. Simmer the saucepan ingredients for 5 minutes until the sauce is bubbly. If the sauce isn't thick enough, mix 1 tablespoon of cornstarch with ½ cup of water, stir and add to the sauce. When the *tortellini* are *al dente* (about 10 minutes), drain with the peas and place in the serving bowl. Pour the cream sauce with the ham and other ingredients over the *tortellini*. Add the nutmeg and cinnamon. Mix well taking care not to tear the *tortellini*. Top with grated *parmigiano* cheese. Serve with extra grated cheese on the side.

Tortellini alla Panna, Peperoni e Pollo- *Tortellini* pasta in pink cream sauce with red peppers and grilled chicken.

Preparation Time: 40 minutes

Ingredients:

- 1 pound of fresh cheese-filled Tortellini or dried variety of the same
- 1 small sweet onion, diced
- 2 whole garlic cloves, minced
- 1 red pepper or roasted red peppers in a jar (*Sun of Italy* brand is inexpensive and good)
- 2 boneless chicken breasts, pounded flat and cut into 2-inch by 1/2-inch strips.
- 1 cup of flour
- 4 tablespoons of unsalted butter
- 2 pints of heavy cream or substitute with white sauce (see *besciamella* recipe on page 22)
- 1 (14.5) ounce can of crushed tomatoes
- 4 tablespoon of olive oil
- 1 pinch of dried sage
- 1 Knorr®'s chicken bouillon cube
- salt and white pepper to taste
- 1 cup of *parmigiano-reggiano* cheese

Fill a 10-quart saucepan with water over high heat for the pasta. Add the pasta during the last 10 minutes of the preparation process to the boiling water. If you don't have the roasted red peppers in a jar, take the whole red pepper and place under a broiler, charring the skin. Remove from the broiler, rinse under cold water and remove the skin using a paring knife. De-seed and de-rib the pepper and slice into thin strips. Set the peppers aside on a plate. Pre-heat a saucepan with the olive oil. Dust the chicken strips in flour. Add the chicken strips, onion, garlic, sage and sauté for 5 minutes. Add the crushed tomatoes and bouillon and simmer for 10 additional minutes. If you can't find heavy cream at the grocery store, make a *besciamella* sauce (see page 22). Add the heavy cream or white sauce to the sautéed tomato sauce ingredients. Add the red pepper strips to the cooked ingredients. Simmer the saucepan ingredients until the cream sauce is bubbly and hot. When the *tortellini* are *al dente* (about 10 minutes), place in the serving bowl. Pour the cream sauce with the chicken and other ingredients over the *tortellini*. Mix well, taking care not to tear the *tortellini*. Top with grated *parmigiano* cheese. Serve with extra grated *parmigiano* cheese on the side.

Tortellini col Pollo e Broccoli (chicken and broccoli)

Preparation Time: 40 minutes

Ingredients:

- 1 pound of cheese-filled fresh Tortellini or dried variety of the same
- 1 fresh head of broccoli, pared into florets (save or discard stems)
- 2 boneless chicken breasts pounded flat and cut into 2-inch by 1/2-inch strips
- 1 cup of flour
- 2 pints of heavy cream or substitute with white sauce (see *besciamella* sauce recipe on page 22)
- 2 whole garlic cloves, minced
- 8 tablespoons of olive oil or as needed
- 1 cup of dry white wine
- 1 Knorr®'s chicken bouillon cube
- salt and pepper to taste
- 1 cup of *parmigiano-reggiano cheese*

Fill a 10-quart saucepan with water over high heat for the pasta. Add the pasta during the last 10 minutes of the preparation process to the boiling water. Steam the broccoli florets for 10 minutes or cook with the pasta. Dust the chicken strips in flour. In a pre-heated saucepan with the olive oil, add the chicken strips, and garlic and sauté for 5 minutes or until the chicken is firm. De-glaze the pan with the white wine and crushed bouillon. If you can't find heavy cream at the grocery store, make a *besciamella* sauce (see recipe on page 22). Add the heavy cream to the sautéed chicken strips. Simmer the cream sauce for 10 minutes while cooking the pasta. If the sauce doesn't thicken enough add one tablespoon of cornstarch to a ½ cup of water, stir, and add it to the sauce. Continue stirring the sauce that should be bubbling hot. Cook the *tortellini* until *al dente*. Transfer the *tortellini* and broccoli to a large serving bowl. Pour the cream sauce with the chicken over the *tortellini* and broccoli. Mix well, taking care not to tear the *tortellini*. Top with grated *parmigiano-reggiano* cheese. Serve with extra grated cheese on the side.

Fettuccine con la Salsiccia, Zucchini e Fagioli Verde- Mild Italian
sausage, green summer squash or zucchini, and green beans with chopped
tomatoes.

Preparation Time: 30 minutes

Ingredients:

- 1 pound of Fettuccine (half-green spinach if available)
- 1/4 pound or 2 medium sized zucchini, cubed
- 1/2 pound of green beans
- 1 (28) ounce or 1 pound 12 ounce can of whole Italian plum tomatoes, drained and diced
- 2 (two) medium-sized mild Italian sausage links (removed from casing)
- 4 tablespoons of olive oil
- 1/4 cup of fresh Italian flat-leaf parsley, chopped
- 3 whole garlic cloves, minced
- 1 small onion, minced
- 1 Knorr®'s chicken bouillon cube

Start the water in a 10-quart saucepan over high heat. Cook the pasta the last 10
minutes of total preparation time. Wash and scrub the zucchini and green beans
and trim off the stem end. Slice the zucchini lengthwise and cut into cubes.
Meanwhile pre-heat a saucepan over medium heat, adding the olive oil when hot.
Add the garlic and onions and *soffriggere* or lightly fry for a few minutes. Add the
sausage removed from its casing and sauté until the meat is browned. Remove the
meat and onion/garlic mixture with a slotted spoon and set aside. If needed add
more olive oil to the saucepan. Add the sliced zucchini and green beans sautéing
until the zucchini are still crisp but slightly browned. Add the chopped tomatoes,
parsley, the bouillon, cooked sausage and onion/garlic mixture that had been set
aside and simmer for 10 minutes. Combine the drained *al dente* pasta with the
zucchini and tomatoes in the saucepan. Toss/mix the ingredients. Place the
completed dish in a large serving bowl. Top with *parmigiano* cheese and a little
parsley for garnish.

variations: 1) use 2 tablespoons of dried basil or 1/3 cup torn basil (chopping
bruises the basil turning the leaves black). 2) add mushrooms to the dish when
adding the tomatoes. 3) low fat version: omit sausage and this is a superb vegetable
dish.

Spaghetti alla Carbonara- This is a classic dish served throughout Italy but is a specialty of the mountainous Abruzzi region and also Rome. This dish is uses raw eggs but you can use "eggbeaters". *Carbonara* means coal miner reflecting an occupation of the mountainous Abruzzi region.

Preparation Time: 30 minutes

Ingredients:

- 1 pound of Spaghetti or tubular pasta such as Penne or Ziti
- 1/4 pound of *pancetta*, or bacon, chopped
- 6 eggs, or 1 carton of pasteurized egg substitute (like *egg-beaters)*
- 2 cups of grated *parmigiano* cheese
- 1 tablespoon of olive oil
- 1 pint of heavy cream or substitute with the *besciamella* sauce (see page 22 for the recipe)
- 1 Knorr®'s chicken bouillon cube

Fill a 10-quart saucepan with water over high heat for the pasta. Add the pasta during the last 10 minutes of the preparation process to the boiling water. Pre-heat a saucepan with the olive oil. Add the cubed bacon or *pancetta* and sauté until the bacon is browned and firm but not crispy (3-4 minutes). Use a slotted spoon to remove the bacon. Allow the saucepan to cool down. Add the heavy cream and bouillon and simmer an additional 5 minutes. Re-add the bacon to the cream sauce. Meanwhile in a mixing bowl combine the grated cheese and the eggs and whisk until the eggs and cheese are thoroughly combined. As soon as the pasta is *al dente*, drain and mix the pasta with the cheese and egg batter. Pour the cream sauce/bacon mixture over the pasta/cheese mixture. Mix well. Transfer the completed dish to a large serving bowl. Serve with grated *parmigiano* cheese apart as well.

variation: use only 3 tablespoons of heavy cream to make a lighter version.

Spaghetti alla Carretiera- Another classic dish which combines bacon or *pancetta* and tuna. I always use Italian canned tuna because it adds significant quality to the dish. As far as the bacon is concerned you can use Canadian bacon or a high quality American bacon with more meat and less fat to substitute for *pancetta*.

Preparation Time: 30 minutes

Ingredients:

- 1 pound of Spaghetti or tubular pasta such as Penne or Ziti
- 1/4 pound of *pancetta*, or bacon, chopped
- 1 can of Italian canned tuna
- 2 whole garlic cloves, minced
- 1/4 pound *porcini* mushrooms or substitute with 1/4 pound of button mushrooms, sliced
- 1 cup of grated *parmigiano* cheese
- 2 tablespoons of olive oil
- 1 Knorr®'s beef bouillon cube or *porcini* mushroom bouillon cube
- 1 cup of water

Fill a 10-quart saucepan with water over high heat for the pasta. Add the pasta during the last 10 minutes of the preparation process to the boiling water. Pre-heat a saucepan and add the olive oil when hot. Add the minced garlic, the bacon cut into little strips and the cleaned and sliced mushrooms to the saucepan. Sauté for a few minutes until the bacon is firm. Add the tuna to the saucepan, breaking it up with a wooden spoon. Add the beef bouillon cube and water. Reduce the heat and simmer this combination for 3 minutes. Meanwhile cook the pasta *al dente* and drain. Toss with the saucepan ingredients. Transfer the completed dish to a large serving bowl. Serve with grated *parmigiano* cheese apart.

Penne all' Arrabbiata- A classic dish which differs from the *Matriciana* sauce because it has more tomatoes and adds hot peppers or hot pepper flakes to give it an extra kick. *Arrabbiata* means "angry" in Italian. As far as the bacon is concerned you can use Canadian bacon or a high quality American bacon with more meat and less fat or Virginia country ham to substitute for *pancetta*.

Preparation Time: 30 minutes

Ingredients:

- 1 pound of tubular pasta such as Penne or Ziti
- 1/4 pound of *pancetta*, or bacon, chopped
- 1 small sweet onion, diced
- 2 whole garlic cloves, minced
- 1 (28) ounce or one pound 12-ounce can of crushed tomatoes or whole canned plum tomatoes, diced
- 2 tablespoons of olive oil
- pinch of hot pepper flakes or *peperoncini,* chopped
- 1/2 Knorr®'s beef bouillon cube

Fill a 10-quart saucepan with water over high heat for the pasta. Add the pasta during the last 10 minutes of the preparation process to the boiling water. Pre-heat a saucepan and add the olive oil when hot. Add the minced garlic, onion and the bacon cut into little strips and sauté for a few minutes until the bacon is firm and slightly browned. Add the beef bouillon, hot pepper flakes or cayenne pepper and the tomatoes. Simmer this combination for 10 minutes. Meanwhile cook the pasta *al dente* and drain. Toss or mix the pasta with the saucepan ingredients. Transfer the completed dish to a large serving bowl. Serve with grated *parmigiano* and *pecorino* cheese apart.

Penne alla Marsala di Lusso- A very rich dish which combines the *"secondo piatto"* of a popular main course veal, chicken or turkey breast *"Marsala"* with a creamy rich sauce over Penne noodles or any pasta of your choice.

Preparation Time: 30 minutes

Ingredients:

- 1 pound of tubular pasta such as Penne or Ziti
- 1 package of boneless chicken or turkey breast (4 or 5 fillets) cut into strips
- 1 cup of flour
- 1 carton of white button mushrooms, sliced (or 15 mushrooms)
- 1 cup of *Marsala* wine, sweet or dry
- 1/2 of an onion, diced
- 2 whole garlic cloves, minced
- 1 quart or 2 pints of heavy cream or make a *besciamella* sauce (see recipe on page 22)
- 4 tablespoons of olive oil or as needed
- 1/4 cup of fresh Italian flat-leaf parsley, chopped
- 1 Knorr®'s chicken bouillon cube

Fill a 10-quart saucepan with water over high heat for the pasta. Add the pasta after the water reaches a boil, approximately 10 minutes before the final preparation of the recipe. Pre-heat a saucepan with 2 tablespoons of olive oil. Add the minced garlic and onion and *soffriggere* or lightly fry for a few minutes. Add the cleaned, sliced mushrooms and parsley to the pan and sauté for 5 minutes. Meanwhile cut the chicken or turkey into 1 inch wide by 2-3 inch long strips. Season the chicken strips with salt and pepper, and then dust the fillets in flour. Remove the mushrooms and parsley with a slotted spoon and place aside in a bowl. Add the other 2 tablespoons of olive oil to the pan and heat until hot. Add the chicken or turkey strips sautéing until the fillets are slightly browned on both sides (no more than 5 minutes). Remove the chicken strips from the pan and place aside on a plate. Turn up the heat to high and add the cup of *Marsala* wine and the crushed bouillon cube. De-glaze the pan over high heat. Scrape the pan with the wooden spoon. Add the heavy cream stirring the mixture until smooth. Reduce the heat to medium, re-add the mushrooms and chicken to the mixture and cook an additional few minutes. To make a thicker sauce, dissolve 1 tablespoon of cornstarch in ½ cup of water. Mix well and add to the sauce. Meanwhile cook the pasta *al dente* and drain. Toss or /mix the pasta with the saucepan ingredients. Top with grated *parmigiano* cheese.

Pasta Portabella- A tomato cream sauce with *Portabella* mushrooms and chicken or turkey breasts is a family favorite.

Preparation Time: 30 minutes

Ingredients:

- 1 pound of tubular pasta such as Rigatoni, Penne, or Ziti
- 1 package of boneless chicken or turkey breast fillets, pounded flat between wax paper
- 2 large *portabella* mushroom caps, sliced
- 1 (14.5) ounce can of crushed tomatoes
- 2 whole garlic cloves, minced
- 1 pint of heavy cream
- 7 tablespoons of olive oil or as needed
- 1/4 cup of fresh Italian flat-leaf parsley, chopped
- 1 Knorr®'s chicken bouillon cube
- 1 cup of dry white wine

Fill a 10-quart saucepan with water over high heat for the pasta. Add the pasta during the last 10 minutes of the preparation process to the boiling water. Pre-heat a saucepan and add 2 tablespoons of the olive oil along with the can of tomatoes. Simmer this apart over medium heat while preparing the other ingredients. Pre-heat another saucepan with 2 tablespoons of olive oil. Add the minced garlic and *soffriggere* or lightly fry until the garlic takes on a little color. Add the cleaned, sliced mushrooms and parsley to the pan and sauté for 5 minutes. Remove the mushrooms and parsley with a slotted spoon and place aside in a bowl. Add the other 3 tablespoons of olive oil to the pan and heat until hot. Add the chicken or turkey breast sautéing until the fillets are slightly browned on both sides (no more than 5 minutes). Remove the chicken from the pan and place aside on a plate. Turn up the heat to high and de-glaze the saucepan with the white wine and the crushed bouillon cube, scraping the saucepan with the wooden spoon. Add the heavy cream stirring the mixture until smooth. Add the tomato sauce mixture to the same pan. Reduce the heat to medium, re-add the mushrooms and chicken to the mixture and cook an additional few minutes. To make a thicker sauce, dissolve 1 tablespoon of cornstarch in ½ cup of water. Mix well and add to the sauce. Meanwhile cook the pasta *al dente* and drain. Transfer the pasta to a large serving bowl or platter. Pour the tomato/cream sauce over the pasta and mix well. Arrange the chicken fillets on top of the dish. Serve with grated *parmigiano* cheese apart.

The author, middle w/ white sweater and Mom in tan raincoat along with our cousins (cugini) the Simeone family in Cisternino, province of Brindisi, Italy.

Ravioli alla Panna e Pollo- Cheese-stuffed Ravioli in tomato cream sauce with *Portabella* mushrooms and chicken or turkey breasts.

Preparation Time: 30 minutes

Ingredients:

- 1 pound of cheese-stuffed Ravioli
- 1 package of boneless chicken or turkey breast fillets, pounded flat between wax paper
- 1 cup of flour
- 1 large *portabella* mushroom cap, sliced
- 1 (14.5) ounce can of crushed tomatoes
- 2 whole garlic cloves, minced
- 2 pints of heavy cream or substitute *besciamella* sauce (recipe on page 22)
- 8 tablespoons of olive oil or as needed
- 1/4 cup of fresh Italian flat-leaf parsley, chopped
- 1 Knorr®'s chicken bouillon cube
- 1 cup of dry white wine

Fill a 10-quart saucepan with water over high heat for the pasta. Add the pasta during the last 4 minutes of the preparation process to the boiling water. Pre-heat a saucepan and add 2 tablespoons of the olive oil along with the can of tomatoes. Simmer this apart over medium heat while preparing the other ingredients. Pre-heat another saucepan with the other 2 tablespoons of olive oil. Add the minced garlic, sliced mushrooms and parsley and *soffriggere* or lightly fry until the garlic takes on a little color. Remove the mushrooms and parsley with a slotted spoon and place aside in a bowl. Add the other 4 tablespoons of olive oil to the pan and heat until hot. Quickly dust the fillets in flour. Sauté the chicken or turkey breast until the fillets are slightly browned on both sides (no more than 5 minutes). Remove the chicken from the pan and place aside on a plate. Turn up the heat to high and add the white wine and the crushed bouillon cube to the saucepan. De-glaze the pan by scraping the pan with the wooden spoon. Add the heavy cream stirring the mixture until smooth. Add the tomato sauce mixture to the same pan. Reduce the heat to medium, re-add the mushrooms and chicken to the mixture and cook an additional few minutes. To make a thicker sauce, dissolve 1 tablespoon of cornstarch in water. Mix well and add to the sauce. Meanwhile cook the pasta *al dente* and drain. Transfer the pasta to a large serving bowl or platter. Pour over the sauce and mix well. Arrange the fillets on top of the pasta. Serve with grated *parmigiano* cheese apart.

Tagliatelle con Melanzane e Salsicce- An Apulian dish which combines eggplant and sausage.

Preparation Time: 30 minutes

Ingredients:

- 1 pound of Tagliatelle
- 1/2 pound of sweet Italian sausage, removed from casing
- 1/4 pound or 4 ounces of bacon or Canadian bacon, diced
- 1 (14.5) ounce can of diced tomatoes
- 1 small sweet onion, diced
- 2 whole garlic cloves, minced
- 2 medium-sized eggplants or 1 large eggplant, diced
- 4 tablespoons of olive oil
- 1/4 cup of fresh Italian flat-leaf parsley, chopped
- sage, fresh leaves chopped or 1 teaspoon of dried sage
- 1 Knorr®'s chicken bouillon cube

Fill a 10-quart saucepan with water over high heat for the pasta. Add the pasta during the last 10 minutes of the preparation process to the boiling water. Pre-heat a saucepan with the 4 tablespoons of olive oil. Add the minced garlic and onion and *soffriggere* or lightly fry for a few minutes. Add the diced eggplant and bacon sauté for 5 to 8 minutes. Meanwhile remove the casing from the sausage adding the filling to the saucepan and sauté an additional 5 minutes. Finally add the tomatoes with liquid, parsley, sage and bouillon cube, allowing the sauce to simmer for 10 minutes. Meanwhile cook the pasta *al dente* and drain. Toss with the saucepan ingredients. Transfer the completed dish to a large serving bowl. Serve with grated *parmigiano* cheese apart.

Spaghetti con Gorgonzola e Pancetta- Gorgonzola cheese and Italian *pancetta* (or substitute Canadian bacon) make this a quick and tasty recipe.

Preparation Time: 30 minutes

Ingredients:

- 1 pound of Spaghetti or other pasta
- 1/4 pound of *pancetta* or Canadian Bacon, chopped
- 1/4 stick of butter
- 1 pint of heavy cream or make a *beciamella* sauce (see recipe on page 22) if heavy cream isn't available
- 1/4 pound of gorgonzola cheese, cut into *julienne* strips
- pinch of cayenne pepper or hot pepper flakes
- 4 tablespoons of olive oil
- salt and white pepper to taste

Fill a 10-quart saucepan with water over high heat for the pasta. Add the pasta during the last 10 minutes of the preparation process to the boiling water. Pre-heat a saucepan with the 4 tablespoons of olive oil. Add the pepper flakes or cayenne pepper and the *pancetta* bacon and sauté for 5 minutes until the bacon is firm. Cut the *gorgonzola* into little match stick pieces or julienne strips. Add the cheese to the saucepan and simmer until the cheese becomes creamy and bubbly. Add the heavy cream and butter and allow these ingredients to blend with the other ingredients. Use a wooden spoon to stir the ingredients. Meanwhile cook the pasta *al dente* and drain. Toss with the saucepan ingredients. Transfer the completed dish to a large serving bowl. Serve with grated *parmigiano* cheese apart.

Penne all'Olive- An Apulian dish which combines the tasty olives of the region with *prosciutto*.

Preparation Time: 30 minutes

Ingredients:

- 1 pound of Penne or other pasta
- 1/4 pound of *prosciutto,* chopped
- 1/2 cup of pitted green *cerignola* olives or pitted black olives such as *gaeta* Italian black olives, minced
- 1 cup of artichokes, chopped
- 1 pint of heavy cream or make a *besciamella* sauce (see recipe on page 22)
- 1 small sweet onion, diced
- 1 (14.5) ounce can of diced tomatoes
- 2 tablespoons of olive oil
- 1/2 of a Knorr®'s vegetable bouillon cube
- 1/2 cup of fresh basil, shredded or torn
- salt and white pepper to taste

Fill a 10-quart saucepan with water over high heat for the pasta. Add the pasta during the last 10 minutes of the preparation process to the boiling water. Pre-heat a saucepan with the 2 tablespoons of olive oil and the butter. Add the onion and a *soffriggere* or lightly fry few minutes. Next add the *prosciutto*, olives, artichokes, basil, 1/2 of a bouillon cube and the diced tomatoes. Simmer over medium heat for 10 minutes. Add the heavy cream and allow the saucepan ingredients to blend. Meanwhile cook the pasta *al dente* and drain. Toss the pasta with the saucepan ingredients. Transfer the completed dish to a large serving bowl. Serve with grated *parmigiano* cheese apart.

Pasta con le Fave e Prosciutto- An Apulian dish which combines popular *fava* bean (found in Italian deli's or specialty health food stores) of the region with *prosciutto.*

Preparation Time: 30 minutes

Ingredients:

- 1 pound of pasta any type
- 1 can of *fava* beans, drained
- 1/4 pound of *prosciutto,* chopped
- 1/4 pound of *pancetta*, or Canadian Bacon or American thick sliced bacon, chopped into small strips
- 4 tablespoons of olive oil
- 1 stalk of celery, diced
- 2 garlic cloves, minced
- 1 small sweet onion, diced
- 1/4 cup of Italian red wine vinegar
- 1 teaspoon of sugar
- salt and white pepper to taste

Fill a 10-quart saucepan with water over high heat for the pasta. Add the pasta during the last 10 minutes of the preparation process to the boiling water. Pre-heat a saucepan with the 4 tablespoons of olive oil. Add the onion, garlic, celery and *pancetta* or bacon and ***soffriggere*** or lightly fry for 5 minutes. Add the *prosciutto* and *fava* beans and simmer for 10 minutes. Add the vinegar and sugar, stir, and simmer for an additional 5 minutes giving the sauce a *dolce-amaro* (bitter-sweet) flavor. Meanwhile cook the pasta *al dente* and drain. Toss with the saucepan ingredients. Transfer the completed dish to a large serving bowl. Serve with grated *pecorino* cheese apart.

Penne con Fagioli e Prosciutto- Apulian dish with fresh green beans and *prosciutto*.

Preparation Time: 30 minutes

Ingredients:

* 1 pound of Penne or other pasta
* 10 ounces or 3/4 pound of fresh or frozen green beans
* 4 ounces or 1/4 pound of *prosciutto*, chopped
* 1 (14.5) ounce can of diced tomatoes
* 4 ounces or 1/4 pound of *pancetta*, or bacon, chopped into small strips
* 1 stick of celery, diced
* 2 whole garlic cloves, minced
* 1 small sweet onion, diced
* 1 small carrot, minced
* 1/2 cup of fresh basil, shredded
* 4 tablespoons of olive oil
* 1/2 of a Knorr®'s vegetable bouillon cube
* 1/2 cup of water
* 1 teaspoon of rosemary or a "pinch"
* salt and white pepper to taste

Fill a 10-quart saucepan with water over high heat for the pasta. Add the pasta during the last 10 minutes of the preparation process to the boiling water. Pre-heat a saucepan with the 4 tablespoons of olive oil. Add the onion, garlic, carrot, celery, and *pancetta* and **soffriggere** or lightly fry for 5 minutes. Meanwhile steam the green beans in a pot or vegetable steamer for 10-12 minutes. Add the *prosciutto,* tomatoes, rosemary, crushed 1/2 bouillon cube, water and basil to the saucepan and simmer for 10 minutes. Add the steamed green beans to the saucepan. Meanwhile cook the pasta *al dente* and drain. Toss the pasta with the saucepan ingredients. Transfer the completed dish to a large serving bowl. Serve with grated *pecorino* cheese apart.

Spaghetti col Vitello alla Puttanesca- The piquant *puttanesca* sauce served over veal cutlets (or chicken breast) combines the first and second course of a fine meal. All you need is bread, wine, and a green salad to make this a complete meal.

Preparation Time: 30 minutes

Ingredients:

- 1 pound of Spaghetti or other pasta
- 1 package of veal scaloppini (or boneless chicken breasts), flattened
- 1 cup of flour
- 1 (28) ounce or one pound, 12 ounce can of crushed tomatoes
- 6 tablespoons of olive oil
- 1/4 cup of black *gaeta* olives or other black olive, pitted and chopped
- 1/4 cup of fresh Italian flat-leaf parsley, chopped
- 4 whole garlic cloves, minced
- 1 small sweet onion, diced
- 2 tablespoons of capers
- 2 flat anchovy fillets (canned)
- 2 tablespoons of clam juice (clam juice from a jar)
- 1/4 stick of butter
- 1/2 of a Knorr®'s chicken bouillon cube

Fill a 10-quart saucepan with water over high heat for the pasta. Add the pasta during the last 10 minutes of the preparation process to the boiling water. Dust the veal fillets in flour and set on a plate. Pre-heat a saucepan over medium heat. Add the butter and some olive oil allowing it to heat up. Take care not to burn the butter. Add the veal fillets to the saucepan and lightly brown the veal on both sides. Don't cook the fillets very long, just a few minutes on both sides. Pre-heat a separate pan over medium heat, add the olive oil and *soffriggere* or lightly fry the garlic, onion and parsley in the olive oil for a few minutes. Add the anchovy fillets and sauté the anchovies until they dissolve. Add the tomatoes, olives and crushed bouillon cube to the saucepan. Simmer all ingredients together for 15 minutes. Transfer the veal fillets to the tomato saucepan ingredients. Add the clam juice, the capers, and the remaining parsley to the saucepan. Cook an additional 5 minutes over medium heat. Combine the drained *al dente* pasta with the saucepan ingredients. Toss/mix well. Transfer the completed dish to a large serving bowl. Place the veal fillets on top of the pasta. Serve with grated *pecorino* and *parmigiano* cheese apart.

Rotini col Pollo e Cavolfiore- Spiral pasta with chicken strips and cauliflower in a cream sauce.

Preparation Time: 30 minutes

Ingredients:

- 1 pound of Rotini or pasta spirals
- 1 fresh head of cauliflower, pared into florets
- 1 package (4-5 chicken breasts)of whole boneless chicken breasts cut into strips
- 1 cup of flour
- salt and pepper to season the flour
- 2 pints or 1 quart of heavy cream or make a *besciamella* sauce (see recipe on page 22)
- 4 tablespoons of olive oil
- 1/2 cup of fresh basil, shredded or torn
- 2 whole garlic cloves, minced
- 1 teaspoon of rosemary or a "pinch"
- 1 Knorr®'s chicken bouillon cube
- 1 cup of grated *mozzarella* or *provolone* cheese (optional)

Fill a 10-quart saucepan with water over high heat for the pasta. Add the pasta during the last 10 minutes of the preparation process to the boiling water. Pre-heat a saucepan with the 2 tablespoons of olive oil. Dust the chicken fillets in flour. Add half of the garlic and all of the chicken and sauté 5 minutes or until the chicken is firm but not overcooked. Meanwhile steam the cauliflower in a pot or vegetable steamer for 10-12 minutes. Remove the chicken from the pan and add the steamed cauliflower with the additional olive oil, garlic, rosemary, basil and the bouillon cube. Crush the bouillon cube with a wooden spoon. Break up the cauliflower. Cook over medium high heat until the cauliflower has a little brown edge. Add the heavy cream to the sauce along with the chicken that was set aside. Simmer an additional 5 minutes or until the sauce is bubbly and hot. To make a thicker sauce, dissolve 1 tablespoon of cornstarch in ½ cup of water. Mix well and add to the sauce. Meanwhile cook the pasta *al dente* and drain. Toss or mix with the saucepan ingredients. Transfer the completed dish to a large serving bowl. Serve with grated *parmigiano* cheese apart. Melt *provolone* or *mozzarella* on the top of the serving dish under the broiler or in the microwave for an added cheese flavor.

Rigatoni col Polpettone- This is the classic meatballs and red sauce. Consistent with the theme of the cookbook, I use pre-cooked *Mama Lucia* brand meatballs added to two cans of crushed tomatoes. Homemade meatballs in Apulia are usually made with minced veal and pork, minced onion, minced garlic, breadcrumbs, *pecorino* cheese, milk, parsley and egg. Breadcrumbs should make up to 30% of the ingredients in order to give the right consistency to the meatballs. Homemade fried or baked meatballs are preferred if you have the time.

Preparation Time: 30 minutes

Ingredients:

- 1 pound of Rigatoni
- 1 pound of frozen *Mama Lucia®* meatballs or homemade with ½ pound of veal or hamburger and ½ pound of pork, ½ minced onion, 2 minced garlic cloves, 2 beaten eggs, 1 cup of breadcrumbs, ½ cup of grated *pecorino* cheese, 4 tablespoons of milk and ½ cup of minced parsley. Soak the breadcrumbs in the milk. Mix all ingredients well with the breadcrumbs. Form golf-ball sized meatballs. Fry in abundant vegetable oil or olive oil.
- 2 whole garlic cloves, minced
- 2 (28 ounce) or 1 pound 12 ounce cans of crushed tomatoes or whole canned plum tomatoes, diced.
- 2 tablespoon of tomato paste
- 4 tablespoons of olive oil
- 1 teaspoon of dried thyme
- 1 teaspoon of dried oregano
- 1 Knorr®'s beef bouillon cube (optional)

Fill a 10-quart saucepan with water over high heat for the pasta. Add the pasta during the last 10 minutes of the preparation process to the boiling water. Pre-heat a saucepan with the olive oil. *Soffriggere* or lightly fry the minced garlic for a few minutes. Add the beef bouillon, thyme, oregano and the tomatoes. Reduce this combination for 10 minutes over medium high heat. Add the pound of meatballs and simmer for 20 minutes until the meatballs are thoroughly heated. (if using homemade meatballs fry in olive oil, dry on paper towels and add to the sauce) Meanwhile cook the pasta *al dente* and drain. Toss or mix the pasta with the saucepan ingredients. Transfer the completed dish to a large serving bowl. Serve with grated *parmigiano* and *pecorino* cheese apart.

Pasta con Scaloppini Pugliese- A very rich dish which combines the *"secondo piatto"* of a popular main course. You can use either veal, chicken or turkey breast in a white wine sauce with eggplant served over flat-ribbon noodles such as *fettuccine* or *tagliatelle* and topped with melted provolone cheese. I prefer to use chicken breast because good veal is difficult to find.

Preparation Time: 40 minutes

Ingredients:

- 1 pound of ribbon pasta such as Tagliatelle
- 1 package of 4 veal scaloppini (or boneless chicken or turkey breast fillets)
- 1 cup of flour
- salt and pepper to season the flour
- 1 medium sized eggplant, cut lengthwise in 1/8 inch slices (very thin)
- 4 slices of *provolone* cheese
- 1/2 stick of butter
- 2 whole garlic cloves, minced
- 6 tablespoons of olive oil or as needed
- 1/4 cup of fresh Italian flat-leaf parsley, chopped
- 1 Knorr®'s chicken bouillon cube
- 1 cup of dry white wine or water

Fill a 10-quart saucepan with water over high heat for the pasta. Add the pasta during the last 10 minutes of the preparation process to the boiling water. Pre-heat a saucepan with 3 tablespoons of olive oil. Add the minced garlic and *soffriggere* or lightly fry until the garlic takes on a little color. Add the chopped parsley and the thinly sliced eggplant to the pan. Sauté the eggplant until browned lightly on both sides. Remove the eggplant and set aside in a plate. Meanwhile dust the fillets (or scaloppini) of thin veal (pound with a mallet if needed) in flour. Add the other 3 tablespoons of olive oil to the pan and the butter. Heat over medium high heat until the oil/butter mix is hot. Add the veal scaloppini and sauté until the fillets are slightly browned on both sides (no more than 5 minutes). Remove the veal and place aside on a plate. Turn up the heat to high and add the cup of dry white wine and the chicken bouillon cube. Crush the bouillon cube with a wooden spoon. Deglaze the contents of the pan by scraping the pan with the wooden spoon. Re-add the veal and eggplant to the dish and keep warm. Meanwhile cook the pasta *al dente* and drain. Combine the pasta with the saucepan ingredients. Arrange the eggplant and veal fillets on top of the pasta. Transfer the completed dish to a large serving dish. Drizzle a little olive oil on top. Add the *provolone* cheese on top of the completed dish and melt under a broiler. Serve with grated *parmigiano* cheese apart.

Pasta col Porchetta Pugliese- Pork chops or pork filet is substituted for pork roast or *porchetta*. This is a very rich dish that combines the *"secondo piatto"* of a popular main course of pork with zucchini and white button mushrooms over pasta.

Preparation Time: 40 minutes

Ingredients:

- 1 pound of Rotini (pasta twists) or pasta any type
- 1 package of 4 to 5 boneless pork cutlets, cut into 2 inch strips
- 1 cup of flour
- 1 teaspoon or a pinch each of thyme, rosemary and sage
- 1 (14.5) ounce can of diced tomatoes
- 3 medium sized zucchini or green squash, sliced
- 15 small white button mushrooms cleaned and sliced
- 1/2 stick of butter
- 2 whole garlic cloves, minced
- 6 tablespoons of olive oil or as needed
- 1/4 cup of fresh Italian flat-leaf parsley, chopped
- 1 Knorr®'s chicken bouillon cube
- salt and pepper to taste

Fill a 10-quart saucepan with water over high heat for the pasta. Add the pasta during the last 10 minutes of the preparation process to the boiling water. Pre-heat a saucepan with 2 tablespoons of olive oil. Add a 1/4 stick of butter along with the garlic, parsley, zucchini and mushrooms to the saucepan. Sauté the zucchini and mushrooms for about 5 minutes until the zucchini are cooked yet still firm. Add the tomatoes with liquid and the crushed chicken bouillon cube to the saucepan. Continue simmering the zucchini, tomato and mushroom mixture. Meanwhile season the pork strips with the thyme, rosemary, sage, salt and pepper and then dust the pork strips in flour. In another saucepan add the other 4 tablespoons of olive oil and butter to the pan and heat over medium high heat until the oil/butter mix is hot. Add the pork strips and sauté until the fillets are slightly browned on both sides and cooked through. Remove the pork strips and place them in the saucepan with the zucchini, tomato and mushroom mixture. Meanwhile cook the pasta *al dente* and drain. Combine the pasta with the saucepan ingredients. Mix and toss well. Transfer the completed dish to a large serving bowl or platter. Arrange the pork strips on top of the pasta. Serve with grated *parmigiano* cheese apart.

Pasta col Vitello Parmigiano-This is a very rich dish which combines the *"secondo piatto"* of a popular main course veal, in a white wine sauce with *parmigiano* cheese and topped with melted *mozzarella* cheese.

Preparation Time: 40 minutes

Ingredients:

- 1 pound of Spaghetti or Linguine
- 1 package of 4 veal scaloppini (boneless veal cutlet pounded flat) or turkey
- 1 cup of flour
- 2 cups of grated *parmigiano* cheese
- 6 tablespoons of olive oil or as needed
- 1/2 stick of butter
- 2 whole garlic cloves, minced
- 1/4 cup of fresh Italian flat-leaf parsley, chopped
- 1 Knorr®'s chicken bouillon cube
- 1 cup of dry white wine or water
- salt and pepper to taste
- 4 slices of *mozzarella* cheese
- 1 cup of grated quality imported *parmigiano* cheese (*reggiano-parmigiano*)

Fill a 10-quart saucepan with water over high heat for the pasta. Add the pasta during the last 10 minutes of the preparation process to the boiling water. Pre-heat a saucepan with 2 tablespoons of olive oil. *Soffriggere* or lightly fry the minced garlic and parsley for a few minutes. Meanwhile dust the fillets (or scaloppini) of thin veal or turkey in a mixture of flour and grated *parmigiano* cheese. Add the other 4 tablespoons of olive oil to the pan and the butter. Heat over medium high heat until the oil/butter mix is hot. Add the veal scaloppini and sauté until the fillets are slightly browned on both sides (no more than 5 minutes). Remove the veal and place aside on a plate. Turn up the heat to high and add the cup of dry white wine and the chicken bouillon cube. De-glaze the contents of the pan by scraping the pan with the wooden spoon. Re-add the veal to the dish and keep warm.
Meanwhile cook the pasta *al dente* and drain. Combine the pasta with the saucepan ingredients. Toss/mix well. Transfer the completed dish to a large serving bowl or platter. Arrange the veal on top of the pasta. Sprinkle the *parmigiano* cheese on top. Add the *mozzarella* cheese on top of the completed dish and melt under a broiler. Serve with grated *parmigiano* cheese apart.

Gemelli col Pollo ed Asparagi- Spiral pasta with chicken and asparagus in a cream sauce.

Preparation Time: 30 minutes

Ingredients:

- 1 pound of Gemelli or pasta spirals
- 1 can of asparagus tips, drained or 1 bunch of steamed asparagus tips
- 1 package (4-5 breasts) of whole boneless chicken breasts, pounded into thin cutlets, and cut into cubes
- 1 cup of flour
- salt and pepper to season the flour
- 2 pints or 1 quart of heavy cream or make a *besciamella* (see recipe on page 22)
- 2 whole garlic cloves, minced
- 4 tablespoons of olive oil or as needed
- 1 Knorr®'s chicken bouillon cube
- 1 cup of grated mozzarella or provolone cheese (optional)

Fill a 10-quart saucepan with water over high heat for the pasta. Add the pasta during the last 10 minutes of the preparation process to the boiling water. Steam the asparagus tips in a steamer for 10–12 minutes or until tender. Pre-heat a saucepan over medium high heat with the 4 tablespoons of olive oil. Dust the chicken cubes in flour. Add the garlic and the chicken and sauté until the chicken is firm but not overcooked. Add the asparagus tips and turn down the heat to medium. Add the heavy cream and crushed bouillon cube to the chicken and asparagus. (or make a white *besciamella* sauce on pg. 22 if heavy cream isn't available). Simmer for 5 minutes or until the cream is bubbly hot. If the sauce isn't thick enough, add 1 tablespoon of cornstarch to ½ cup of water, stir and add to the sauce. Meanwhile cook the pasta *al dente* and drain. Combine the pasta with the saucepan ingredients. Toss or mix well. Transfer the completed dish to a large serving bowl. Serve with grated *parmigiano* cheese apart. Melt *provolone* or *mozzarella* on the top of the serving dish under the broiler or in the microwave for an added cheese flavor.

Rotini col Pollo e Funghi- Spiral pasta with chopped chicken strips and mushrooms in a red sauce.

Preparation Time: 30 minutes

Ingredients:

- 1 pound of Rotini or pasta spirals
- 1 package of white button mushrooms, sliced
- 1 package (4-5 breasts) of whole boneless chicken breasts cut into strips
- 1 (28) ounce or one pound 12-ounce can of crushed tomatoes or whole canned plum tomatoes, diced
- 1/2 cup of fresh basil, shredded or torn
- 4 whole garlic cloves, minced
- 4 tablespoons of olive oil
- 1 teaspoon of rosemary or a "pinch"
- 1 Knorr®'s chicken bouillon cube
- 1 cup of grated *mozzarella* or *provolone* cheese (optional)
- salt and pepper to taste

Fill a 10-quart saucepan with water over high heat for the pasta. Add the pasta during the last 10 minutes of the preparation process to the boiling water. Pre-heat a saucepan with the 2 tablespoons of olive oil. Add half of the garlic and all of the mushrooms and *soffriggere* or lightly fry for 5 minutes. Add the chicken strips to the saucepan along with the additional olive oil, rosemary, minced garlic and the bouillon cube. Sauté for 3 minutes or until the chicken is cooked through. Add the crushed tomatoes and basil and continue simmering for an additional 10 minutes. Meanwhile cook the pasta *al dente* and drain. Combine the pasta with the saucepan ingredients. Toss or mix well. Transfer the completed dish to a large serving bowl. Serve with grated *parmigiano* cheese apart. Melt *provolone* or *mozzarella* cheese on the top of the serving dish under the broiler or in the microwave for added cheese flavor.

Rotini col Pollo e Ceci- Spiral pasta with chopped chicken, c*eci* beans, mushrooms, zucchini, artichokes and cherry tomatoes. Cherry tomatoes and artichokes abound in *Puglia* and are found in many local dishes.

Preparation Time: 30 minutes

Ingredients:

- 1 pound of Rotini or pasta spirals
- 1 can of *ceci* or garbanzo beans, drained
- 1 package of white button mushrooms, sliced
- 1 (12) ounce can of chunk light chicken, cubed
- 1/2 pound of fresh cherry tomatoes
- 2 small zucchini or green squash, sliced
- 1/2 cup of fresh basil, shredded or torn
- 1 small of can of artichoke hearts, liquid drained and chopped
- 4 whole garlic cloves, minced
- 4 tablespoons of olive oil
- 1 Knorr®'s chicken bouillon cube
- 1 cup of dry white wine or water
- salt and pepper to taste

Fill a 10-quart saucepan with water over high heat for the pasta. Add the pasta during the last 10 minutes of the preparation process to the boiling water. Pre-heat a saucepan with the 4 tablespoons of olive oil. Add the garlic, mushrooms, zucchini and tomatoes, and *soffriggere* or lightly fry for 5 minutes. Add the chopped chicken to the saucepan along with the *ceci* beans, basil, artichokes, bouillon cube and white wine or water. Simmer for 10 minutes. Meanwhile cook the pasta *al dente* and drain. Combine the pasta with the saucepan ingredients. Toss and mix well. Transfer the completed dish to a large serving bowl. Serve with grated *parmigiano* cheese apart. Top with a few fresh basil leaves for garnish.

Tagliatelle con le Vedure e Pancetta- Mixed vegetables and bacon sauce.

Preparation Time: 30 minutes

Ingredients:

- 1 pound of Tagliatelle or other flat noodle
- 3 or 4 slices of thick cut bacon or *pancetta,* chopped
- 10 cherry tomatoes, halved or 6 plum tomatoes, seeded and chopped
- 3/4 cup of artichoke hearts, chopped
- 1 small zucchini, cubed or sliced
- 5 button mushrooms, cleaned and sliced
- 2 whole garlic cloves, minced
- 1 tablespoon of capers
- 2 tablespoons of olive oil
- 1/4 cup of fresh Italian flat-leaf parsley, chopped
- 1 Knorr®'s chicken or vegetable bouillon cube
- 1 cup of dry white wine or water
- salt and white pepper to taste

Fill a 10-quart saucepan with water over high heat for the pasta. Add the pasta during the last 10 minutes of the preparation process to the boiling water. Pre-heat a saucepan with the 2 tablespoons of olive oil. Sauté the minced garlic and the diced bacon until the bacon is firm and browned. Finally add the tomatoes, artichokes, capers, mushrooms, zucchini, parsley, bouillon cube and wine or water to the saucepan. Allow the sauce to simmer for 15 minutes. Meanwhile cook the pasta *al dente* and drain. Combine the pasta with the saucepan ingredients. Toss and mix well. Transfer the completed dish to a large serving bowl. Serve with grated *parmigiano* cheese apart.

Vermicelli con Melanzane- Eggplant, capers and olives are the condiments in this dish.

Preparation Time: 30 minutes

Ingredients:

- 1 pound of Vermicelli or Spaghetti
- 3 anchovy fillets or 1 teaspoon of anchovy paste
- 2 whole garlic cloves, minced
- 1 small eggplant, cubed
- 4 tablespoons of olive oil
- 1 tablespoon of capers
- 4 tomatoes, seeded and chopped or 10 cherry tomatoes halved
- 10 black olives, pitted and diced
- 2 ounces of *prosciutto crudo*, chopped
- 1/4 cup of fresh Italian flat-leaf parsley, chopped
- 1 Knorr®'s vegetable bouillon cube
- 1 cup of dry white wine or water
- salt and pepper to taste

Fill a 10-quart saucepan with water over high heat for the pasta. Add the pasta during the last 10 minutes of the preparation process to the boiling water. Pre-heat a saucepan with the 4 tablespoons of olive oil. *Soffriggere* or lightly fry the minced garlic, anchovies and cubed eggplant for a few minutes. Add the tomatoes, olives, capers, *prosciutto*, parsley, bouillon cube and wine to the saucepan. Allow the sauce to simmer for 10 minutes. Meanwhile cook the pasta *al dente* and drain. Combine the pasta with the saucepan ingredients. Toss and mix well. Transfer the completed dish to a large serving bowl. Serve with grated *pecorino* cheese apart

Penne con Melanzane e Prosciutto Cotto- Penne pasta with eggplant, artichokes and cooked ham.

Preparation Time: 30 minutes

Ingredients:

- 1 pound of Penne or Ziti or other tubular pasta
- 1 (one) inch thick cutlet of cooked ham, chopped into cubes or 4 ounces of cooked ham luncheon meat, rolled and sliced
- 1 small eggplant, diced
- 1 (14.5) ounce can of diced tomatoes
- 2 green onions, minced or 1 small sweet onion, diced
- 3/4 cup of marinated artichokes, chopped
- 2 whole garlic cloves, minced
- 5 black olives, pitted
- 1 tablespoon of capers
- 4 tablespoons of olive oil
- 1/4 cup of fresh Italian flat-leaf parsley, chopped
- 1 Knorr®'s chicken or vegetable bouillon cube
- salt and pepper to taste

Fill a 10-quart saucepan with water over high heat for the pasta. Add the pasta during the last ten minutes of the preparation process to the boiling water. Pre-heat a saucepan with the 4 tablespoons of olive oil. *Soffriggere* or lightly fry the garlic, onion and eggplant for a few minutes. Add the ham, tomatoes, artichokes, olives, capers, parsley and bouillon cube to the saucepan. Allow the sauce to simmer for 10 minutes. Meanwhile cook the pasta *al dente* and drain. Combine the pasta with the saucepan ingredients. Toss and mix well. Transfer the completed dish to a large serving bowl. Serve with grated *parmigiano* or *pecorino* cheese apart.

Farfalle con Ceci e Pancetta- This Apulian dish has the wonderful combination of *ceci* beans and bacon.

Preparation Time: 30 minutes

Ingredients:

- 1 pound of Farfalle
- 1 can of *ceci* or garbanzo beans, pureed with olive oil in a blender or food processor
- 4 slices of thick bacon or *pancetta*, chopped
- 2 ounces of dried *porcini* mushrooms, re-hydrated in water
- 1 tablespoon of tomato paste
- 1 tablespoon of dried rosemary
- 1/4 cup of fresh Italian flat-leaf parsley, chopped
- 4 tablespoons of olive oil
- 2 whole garlic cloves, minced
- 1/2 of a Knorr®'s chicken bouillon cube
- 1 cup of dry white wine or water
- salt and white pepper to taste

Fill a 10-quart saucepan with water over high heat for the pasta. Add the pasta during the last 10 minutes of the preparation process to the boiling water. Prepare the *ceci* beans by pureeing the beans in a food processor with 2 tablespoons of olive oil until thick and creamy. In a heated pan with 2 tablespoons of olive oil, sauté the garlic, mushrooms with liquid reserve, bacon, parsley and rosemary until the bacon is firm and browned. Combine/mix the creamed beans, the tomato paste, bouillon and wine with the saucepan ingredients of mushroom/bacon. Stir and simmer this mixture until hot and bubbly. Meanwhile cook the pasta *al dente* and drain. Combine the pasta with the saucepan ingredients. Toss and mix well. Transfer the completed dish to a large serving bowl. Top with a few tablespoons of *pecorino* cheese. Serve with *parmigiano* and or *pecorino* cheese apart as well.

Farfalle con Spinaci e Prosciutto Cotto- Butterfly pasta, cooked ham, spinach and vegetables round out this dish.

Preparation Time: 30 minutes

Ingredients:

- 1 pound of Farfalle or tubular pasta
- 1 (one) inch thick cutlet of cooked ham, chopped or 4 ounces of ham luncheon meat, rolled and sliced
- 2 cups of frozen chopped spinach or half bag of fresh spinach leaves, stems trimmed
- 1 small zucchini, diced
- 1 (14.5) ounce can of diced tomatoes
- 2 green onions or 1 small sweet onion, diced
- 2 whole garlic cloves, minced
- 1 cup of frozen corn
- 4 tablespoons of olive oil
- 1/4 cup of fresh Italian flat-leaf parsley, chopped
- 1 Knorr®'s chicken bouillon cube
- 1 cup of dry white wine or water
- salt and white pepper to taste

Fill a 10-quart saucepan with water over high heat for the pasta. Add the pasta during the last 10 minutes of the preparation process to the boiling water. Pre-heat a saucepan with the 4 tablespoons of olive oil. *Soffriggere* or lightly fry the garlic, onion and zucchini for a few minutes. Add the ham, tomatoes, spinach, corn, parsley, bouillon cube and wine to the saucepan. Allow the sauce to simmer for 10 minutes. Meanwhile cook the pasta *al dente* and drain. Combine the pasta with the saucepan ingredients. Toss and mix well. Transfer the completed dish to a large serving bowl. Serve with grated *parmigiano* cheese

Orecchiette con Salsiccie e Vedure- An Apulian dish which combines broccoli and sausage.

Preparation Time: 30 minutes

Ingredients:

- 1 pound of Orecchiette (in your Italian deli or substitute any other pasta)
- 1 pound of sweet Italian sausage, squeeze out of the casing
- 1 head of broccoli, pared into florets
- 1 small sweet onion, minced.
- 2 whole garlic cloves, diced
- 4 tablespoons of olive oil
- 1/4 cup of fresh Italian flat-leaf parsley, chopped
- 1 Knorr®'s chicken bouillon cube
- 1 cup of dry white wine or water
- salt and pepper to taste

Fill a 10-quart saucepan with water over high heat for the pasta. Add the pasta during the last 10 minutes of the preparation process to the boiling water. Pre-heat a saucepan with the 4 tablespoons of olive oil. *Soffriggere* or lightly fry the minced garlic and onion for a few minutes. Meanwhile remove the casing from the sausage. Add the meat filling to the saucepan and sauté until browned. Add the broccoli florets and *soffriggere* or lightly fry for 5 to 8 minutes. Finally add the wine, parsley and crushed bouillon cube and allow the sauce to simmer for 5 minutes. Add more olive oil if needed. Meanwhile cook the pasta *al dente* and drain. Combine the pasta with the saucepan ingredients. Toss and mix well. Transfer the completed dish to a large serving bowl. Serve with grated *pecorino* cheese apart.

Cavatidd con Ragu' di Agnello- An Apulian dish that combines eggplant and lamb Ragu'. *Cavatidd* is Cisternino dialect for *Cavatelli* pasta.

Preparation Time: 40 minutes

Ingredients:

- 1 pound of Cavatelli or Tagliatelle or any other pasta on-hand
- 1 pound of boneless lamb, cut into small cubes
- 2 tablespoons of tomato paste
- 1 (28 ounce) or 1 pound 12 ounce can of crushed tomatoes or whole canned plum tomatoes, diced
- 1 small sweet onion, diced
- 2 whole garlic cloves, minced
- 1 medium eggplant, diced
- 6 tablespoons of olive oil or as needed
- 1/4 cup of fresh Italian flat-leaf parsley, chopped
- 1 tablespoon of rosemary
- 1 Knorr®'s beef bouillon cube
- 1 cup of dry red wine

Fill a 10-quart saucepan with water over high heat for the pasta. Add the pasta during the last 10 minutes of the preparation process to the boiling water. Pre-heat a saucepan with 4 tablespoons of olive oil. *Soffriggere* or lightly fry the minced garlic, onion and diced eggplant for 5 to 8 minutes. In another pre-heated pan brown the lamb cubes with the rest of the olive oil and rosemary. De-glaze the lamb with the red wine and crushed bouillon cube. Add the lamb to the eggplant, onion and garlic mixture in the saucepan. Finally add the tomatoes, tomato paste, and parsley to the saucepan and allow the sauce to simmer for 30 minutes. Meanwhile cook the pasta *al dente* and drain. Combine the pasta with the saucepan ingredients. Toss and mix well. Transfer the completed dish to a large serving bowl. Serve with grated *pecorino* cheese apart.

Pasta col Vitello Parmigiano al Pomodoro-This is a very rich dish which combines the *"secondo piatto"* of a popular main course veal, in a tomato wine sauce and topped with grated *parmigiano-reggiano or grana padana* cheese.

Preparation Time: 40 minutes

Ingredients:

- 1 pound of Spaghetti or Linguine
- 1 package of 4 veal scaloppini (boneless veal cutlet pounded flat)
- 1 cup of flour
- 1/2 stick of butter
- 2 eggs, beaten to dip the fillets in
- 2 cups of bread crumbs mixed with one cup of *parmigiano* cheese
- 8 tablespoons of olive oil or sufficient vegetable oil to fry fillets
- salt and white pepper to taste

For the tomato sauce:
- 1 (28) ounce or 1 pound 12 ounce can of crushed tomatoes
- 2 whole garlic cloves, minced
- 1/4 cup of fresh Italian flat-leaf parsley, chopped
- 1 Knorr®'s chicken bouillon cube
- 1 cup of dry white wine

Fill a 10-quart saucepan with water over high heat for the pasta. Add the pasta during the last 10 minutes of the preparation process to the boiling water. Pre-heat a saucepan with 6 tablespoons of olive oil and the butter. Meanwhile dust the fillets (or scaloppini) of thin veal (pound with a mallet if needed) in the flour, egg wash and then the bread crumb/cheese mixture until well coated. Sauté the veal scaloppini until the fillets are slightly browned on both sides (no more than 5 minutes). Use oil as needed to fry the fillets in. Remove the veal and place aside on a plate. In a separate saucepan, heat the remaining olive oil and *soffriggere* or lightly fry the minced garlic. Add the crushed bouillon cube and the white wine. Add the crushed tomatoes and parsley to the saucepan. Simmer the saucepan ingredients for 20 minutes. Re-add the veal to the saucepan and keep warm over low heat. Meanwhile cook the pasta *al dente* and drain. Combine the pasta with the saucepan ingredients. Toss and mix well. Transfer the completed dish to a serving bowl. Arrange the veal cutlets on top. Top with *parmigiano* cheese.

Fettuccine con gli Zucchini, Finocchio e Pancetta- Green summer
squash or zucchini with chopped fennel and bacon. Fennel is a commonly used in
Apulia.

Preparation Time: 30 minutes

Ingredients:

- 1 pound of Fettuccine
- 1/2 pound or 4 medium sized zucchini, cubed
- 1 (28) ounce or 1 pound 12 ounce can of whole Italian plum tomatoes, diced
- 1 small fennel bulb, diced (discard stem and frond)
- 1/4 pound of *pancetta* or American bacon, diced
- 4 tablespoons of olive oil
- 1/4 cup of fresh Italian flat-leaf parsley, chopped
- 2 whole garlic cloves, minced
- 1 Knorr®'s vegetable bouillon cube

Start the water in a 10-quart saucepan over high heat. Cook the pasta the last ten
minutes of total preparation time. Wash and scrub the zucchini and trim off the
stem end. Slice the zucchini and cut into cubes. Pre-heat a saucepan over medium
high heat adding the olive oil when hot. Add the bacon, garlic, and fennel and sauté
until the bacon is firm. Add the cubed zucchini sautéing until the zucchini are still
crisp and slightly browned. Add the chopped tomatoes, bouillon and parsley and
simmer for 10 minutes over medium heat. Combine the drained *al dente* pasta with
the zucchini, bacon, fennel and tomatoes in the saucepan. Toss and mix well.
Transfer the completed dish to a large serving bowl. Top with grated *pecorino*
cheese and a little parsley for garnish.

variation: use 2 tablespoons of dried basil or 1/3 cup torn basil. Add mushrooms to
the dish when adding the tomatoes.

Pasta con Braciole di Manzo al Pomodoro- An Apulian dish that my cousins prepared for me. Beef flank steak or top round sliced thinly, stuffed, rolled and simmered in a tomato sauce.

Preparation Time: 40 minutes

Ingredients:

- 1 pound of Ziti or other tubular pasta
- 4 slices of top round or flank steak, 3 ounces or so per slice
- 1 cup of flour
- 1/2 cup of *pecorino* cheese, grated
- 1/4 cup of fresh Italian flat-leaf parsley, minced
- 1 sweet red onion, minced
- 1 Knorr®'s beef bouillon cube
- 1 cup of dry red wine
- 6 tablespoons of olive oil or as needed

For the tomato sauce:
- 1 tablespoon of tomato paste
- 1 (28 ounce) or one pound 12 ounce can of crushed tomatoes or whole canned plum tomatoes, diced
- 2 whole garlic cloves, minced
- 1 cup of pitted green *Cerignola* olives, chopped
- 1 teaspoon of dried oregano
- pinch of hot pepper flakes

Fill a 10-quart saucepan with water over high heat for the pasta. Add the pasta during the last 10 minutes of the preparation process to the boiling water. Pre-heat a saucepan with 2 tablespoons of olive oil. *Soffriggere* or lightly fry the garlic for a few minutes. Add the crushed tomatoes, tomato paste, olives, pepper flakes and oregano and simmer while preparing the *braciole*. In a mixing bowl combine and blend the parsley, red onion and *pecorino* cheese. Dust the *braciole* fillets in flour. Lay the *braciole* fillets out on a flat surface and spread the parsley, red onion and cheese mixture evenly to form a thin layer on the meat fillets. Roll the fillets and secure with butcher's twine or toothpicks. In a heavy skillet brown the *braciole* on all sides and remove them with a slotted spoon to a plate. De-glaze the skillet over high heat with the wine and beef bouillon cube. Make sure to loosen the browned bits with a wooden spoon. Combine the tomato sauce, *braciole* and the *braciole* saucepan ingredients. Simmer the combined ingredients for 20 minutes. Meanwhile cook the pasta *al dente* and drain. Toss and mix the pasta with the saucepan ingredients. Transfer the completed dish to a large serving bowl. Arrange the *braciole* on top. Serve with grated *pecorino* cheese apart.

Spaghetti col Pollo, Zucchini e Pomodori- Chicken, mushrooms, and zucchini with chopped tomatoes.

Preparation Time: 30 minutes

Ingredients:

- 1 pound of Spaghetti or Penne
- 4 boneless chicken breasts, sliced into strips
- 1 cup of flour
- salt and pepper
- 1 cup of vegetable oil for frying chicken
- 1/2 pound or 4 medium-sized zucchini, sliced
- 1 cup of white button mushrooms, sliced
- 1 (14.5) ounce can of diced tomatoes
- 4 tablespoons of olive oil
- 1/4 cup of fresh Italian flat-leaf parsley, chopped
- 1 small green onion, minced
- 2 whole garlic cloves, minced
- 1 Knorr®'s chicken bouillon cube

Fill a 10-quart saucepan with water over high heat for the pasta. Add the pasta after the water reaches a boil, approximately 10 minutes before the final preparation of the recipe. Dust the chicken strips in seasoned flour. Fry the chicken strips in vegetable oil until golden brown. Set the chicken aside on a plate. Wash and scrub the zucchini and trim off the stem end. Slice the zucchini into 1/5-inch disks and cut into half-moons. Pre-heat a saucepan over medium heat adding the olive oil when hot. Add the garlic and onion and *soffriggere* or lightly fry for a few minutes. Add the sliced zucchini, mushrooms, parsley, bouillon, and tomatoes with liquid and simmer all ingredients for 10 minutes. Combine the drained *al dente* pasta with the zucchini, mushrooms and tomatoes in the saucepan. Toss the pasta with the saucepan ingredients. Transfer the completed dish to a large serving bowl. Arrange the chicken on top of the pasta. Top with *parmigiano* cheese and a little parsley for garnish. Serve with grated *parmigiano* cheese apart.

Spaghetti con i Carciofi e Finocchio- Artichokes and fennel are two key vegetables in Apulia.

Preparation Time: 30 minutes

Ingredients:

- 1 pound of Spaghetti
- 1 small fennel bulb, chopped
- 1 can of artichoke hearts, drained and chopped
- 4 ounces of *prosciutto*, chopped
- 4 tablespoons of olive oil
- 1/4 cup of fresh Italian flat-leaf parsley, chopped
- 2 whole garlic cloves, minced
- 1 Knorr®'s vegetable bouillon cube
- 1/2 cup of water

Fill a 10-quart saucepan with water over high heat for the pasta. Add the pasta after the water reaches a boil, approximately 10 minutes before the final preparation of the recipe. Pre-heat a saucepan over medium heat adding the olive oil when hot. Add the garlic and fennel and *soffriggere* or lightly fry until the fennel softens. Add the artichokes, *prosciutto*, bouillon, parsley and 1/2 cup of water and simmer for 10 minutes over medium high heat. Combine the drained *al dente* pasta with the saucepan ingredients. Toss/mix well. Transfer the completed dish to a large serving bowl. Top with *pecorino* cheese and a little parsley for garnish.

variation: use 2 tablespoons of dried basil or 1/3 cup of torn basil.

Spaghetti con i Filetti al Limone- Chicken or Turkey breast fillet with a light lemon-wine sauce. Citrus fruit abounds in Apulia and cooking with lemons is popular.

Preparation Time: 30 minutes

Ingredients:

- 1 pound of Spaghetti
- 1 pound of chicken or turkey scaloppini or pounded fillets
- 1 cup of flour to dust fillets
- Juice of one lemon
- Zest of one lemon
- 1 tablespoon of capers
- 4 tablespoons of olive oil
- 1/4 cup of fresh Italian flat-leaf parsley, chopped
- 2 whole garlic cloves, minced
- 1/2 of a Knorr®'s chicken bouillon cube
- 1 cup of dry white wine or water

Fill a 10-quart saucepan with water over high heat for the pasta. Add the pasta after the water reaches a boil, approximately 10 minutes before the final preparation of the recipe. Pre-heat a saucepan over medium heat adding the olive oil when hot. Add the garlic and *soffriggere* or lightly fry for a few minutes. Dust the chicken or turkey fillets in the flour. Add the chicken or turkey scaloppini fillets to the frying pan and lightly brown on both sides. Remove the fillets from heat and place aside on a plate. Add the capers, bouillon and white wine and de-glaze the frying pan over medium high heat. Scrape any of the browned bits clinging to the pan. Add the lemon juice and zest of the lemon along with the meat fillets back to the pan. Turn down the heat to low. Combine the drained *al dente* pasta with the saucepan ingredients. Place the fillets on top of the pasta. Transfer the completed dish to a large serving bowl. Top with *parmigiano* or *pecorino* cheese and a little parsley for garnish.

variation: use 2 tablespoons of dried basil or 1/3 cup of torn basil. Add hot pepper flakes to make the dish *"arrabbiata"*.

**Vaulted archways of Cisternino. Mortar is used to make the houses
and arches of the town center unlike the *Trulli* houses that are made of
un-mortared stone. The exteriors are impermeable to moisture.**

Seafood-Based Sauces

Pesce e Frutti di Mare

Seafood based sauces are among my favorites however seafood can be expensive. Good Italian cooks are *"furbo" or* sly and know how to cut corners on cost without compromising on flavor. I look for seafood items on-sale like clams, mussels, salmon, shrimp, and scallops. I always have cans of fancy Albacore chunk whole tuna in water and minced canned clams that I often can obtain on-sale. I keep a bottle of clam juice that can be found in most any major grocery store on-hand to impart flavor to pasta dishes. Almost all seafood-based sauces can be prepared from scratch in less than 30 minutes, which is an added bonus.

Dinner with my cousins (*cugini*) the Scarafile's. The author is top row far right along side his brother Rick and cousin Donato Scarafile, our host. He served us *Orrechiette* and *Braciole* or *Involtini* of beef. Seafood served many ways is also a favorite *cibo* or food in the region of Apulia.

106

Linguine con le Vongole in Bianco- Linguine in a clear white clam broth is a very popular dish in our household. It is inexpensive, easy and quick to prepare, and one of the most classic and flavorful of all pasta dishes. Clam sauce is found throughout Italy with many variations, mine of course is suited to the American kitchen. If you can find little neck clams or Mahogany clams that aren't outrageously expensive they can substitute for the Italian *vongola.*

Preparation Time: 20 minutes

Ingredients:

- 1 pound of Linguine
- 2 cans of minced or chopped clams with liquid
- 4 tablespoons of olive oil
- 1/4 cup of fresh Italian flat-leaf parsley, chopped
- 1/4 cup of stuffed olives with pimiento, chopped
- 1 tablespoon of capers
- 4 whole garlic cloves, minced
- 1 cup of dry white wine or water
- 1 Knorr®'s chicken bouillon cube
- salt and pepper to taste

Start the water in a 10-quart saucepan over high heat. Add the pasta to the water as soon as the water begins to boil. Pre-heat a saucepan with the 4 tablespoons of olive oil. *Soffriggere* or lightly fry the garlic for a few minutes. Add the white wine or water, crushed bouillon and olives and simmer for 3 minutes. Add the minced or chopped clams with clam broth liquid, capers and parsley and simmer for an additional 3 minutes. Combine and toss the drained *al dente* pasta with the clam sauce and continue cooking for 1 minute. Transfer the completed dish to a large serving bowl. Top with parsley sprigs for garnish. Grind fresh pepper on top for added flavor and salt to taste. *Per carita', p*lease do not serve this dish with cheese!

Linguine con le Vongole in Rosso- The same clam sauce recipe with a touch of tomato. Don't overwhelm the delicate seafood flavor with too many tomatoes.

Preparation Time: 30 minutes

Ingredients:

- 1 pound of Linguine
- 2 cans of *Gorton's* ® minced or chopped clams with liquid
- 4 tablespoons of olive oil
- 1 (14.5) ounce can of diced plum tomatoes
- 1/4 cup of fresh Italian flat-leaf parsley, chopped
- 1/4 cup of stuffed olives with pimiento, chopped
- 1 tablespoon of capers
- 4 whole garlic cloves, minced
- 1 cup of dry white wine or water
- 1 Knorr®'s chicken bouillon cube
- salt and pepper to taste

Start the water in a 10-quart saucepan under high heat. Add the pasta to the water as soon as the water begins to boil. Pre-heat a saucepan with the 4 tablespoons of olive oil. *Soffriggere* or lightly fry the garlic for a few minutes. Add the white wine or water, bouillon cube and olives and simmer for 3 minutes. Add the tomatoes and simmer for 10 minutes. Add the minced clams with clam broth liquid, capers and parsley to the tomatoes and simmer for an additional 3 minutes. Combine/toss the drained *al dente* pasta with the clam sauce and continue cooking for 1 minute. Transfer the completed dish to a large serving bowl. Top with parsley sprigs for garnish. Grind fresh pepper on top for added flavor and salt to taste. Do not serve with cheese!

Linguine con le Cozze- Mussels that are farm-raised are safe, sweet, and delicious. You can find them in 3 pound bags in the seafood department of most major grocery chains.

Preparation Time: 30 minutes

Ingredients:

- 1 pound of Linguine
- 1 (2-3) pound bag of fresh mussels (cozze)
- 2 tablespoons of olive oil
- 1 (28) ounce or 1 pound 12 ounce can of whole Italian plum tomatoes, drained and diced
- 1/2 cup of fresh Italian flat-leaf parsley, chopped
- 4 whole garlic cloves, minced
- 1 cup of dry white wine or water

Start the water in a 10-quart saucepan over high heat. Cook the pasta the last 10 minutes of total preparation time. Scrub the mussels thoroughly. Remove the "beard" protruding from the shell by pulling it out or by using a paring knife. Place the mussels in a bowl and rinse the mussels 2-3 times with cold water to remove any sediment. Discard any mussels that remain open after prodding the inside with a knife. Pre-heat a saucepan with the 2 tablespoons of olive oil. Add 1/2 of the garlic, and *soffriggere* or lightly fry in olive oil until the garlic takes on a little color. Add the drained mussels, parsley and white wine and cook over medium high heat with a lid over the saucepan until the mussels open. Remove the mussels with a slotted spoon and reserve the liquid in a separate bowl. Discard any unopened cooked mussels. Strain the mussel juice after allowing any sediment to settle to the bottom of the bowl. Pre-heat a saucepan again and add the olive oil and garlic. *Soffriggere* or lightly fry the garlic for a few minutes. Add the canned tomatoes to the saucepan and simmer for 10 minutes. Meanwhile add the pasta to the water. Re-add the mussels and the strained mussel liquid to the tomatoes and simmer for 5 minutes. Combine the drained *al dente* pasta with the mussels and tomato sauce in the saucepan. Toss and mix the pasta with the saucepan ingredients. Transfer the completed dish to a large serving bowl. Arrange the mussels around the bowl or platter on top of the pasta. Top with parsley sprigs for garnish. Grind fresh pepper on top for added flavor and salt to taste. Do not serve with cheese!

Linguine Sapore di Mare- This dish marries different *frutti di mare* or "fruits of the sea" with a touch of tomato for an elegant special occasion dish.

Preparation Time: 45 minutes

Ingredients:

- 1 pound of Linguine
- 1 pound of fresh mussels
- 1 can of *Gorton's®* minced or chopped clams w/ liquid
- 1/4 pound of sea scallops
- 1 pound of medium sized or larger shrimp, shelled and de-veined
- 1/4 pound of cleaned *calamari* or squid cut into rings
- 2 tablespoons of olive oil
- 1 (28) ounce or 1 pound 12 ounce can of whole Italian plum tomatoes, drained and diced
- 1/2 cup of fresh Italian flat-leaf parsley, chopped
- 4 whole garlic cloves, minced
- 1 cup of dry white wine or water

Start the water in a 10-quart saucepan over high heat. Cook the pasta the last 10 minutes of total preparation time. Scrub the mussels thoroughly. Remove the "beard" protruding from the shell by pulling it out or by using a paring knife. Place the mussels in a bowl and rinse the mussels 2-3 times with cold water to remove any sediment. Discard any mussels that remain open after prodding the inside with a knife. Pre-heat a saucepan with the 2 tablespoons of olive oil. Add 1/2 of the garlic, and *soffriggere* or lightly fry in olive oil for a few minutes. Add the drained mussels and white wine and cook over medium high heat with a lid over the pan for until the mussels open. Remove the mussels with a slotted spoon and reserve the liquid in a separate bowl. Discard any unopened cooked mussels. Strain the mussel juice after allowing any sediment to settle to the bottom of the bowl. Pre-heat the saucepan again, add the olive oil and *soffriggere* or lightly fry the garlic for a few minutes. Add the shrimp, scallops and *calamari* and sauté until the seafood turns white and firm (just a few minutes). Add the diced tomatoes, canned clams with liquid and parsley to the saucepan and simmer for 5 minutes. Meanwhile add the pasta to the water. Re-add the mussels and the strained mussel juice to the tomato/seafood sauce and warm over low heat for 3 minutes. Combine the drained *al dente* pasta with the mussels and tomato/seafood sauce in the saucepan and cook for 2 minutes. Toss and mix all ingredients. Transfer the completed dish to a large serving bowl. Top with parsley sprigs for garnish.

110

The thick limestone walls of the *Trulli* houses are ideal for the very arid and hot summers of *Puglia*. The temperature inside the *Trulli* are consistent year-round in the 60's ° F range.

Linguine al Salmone Affumicato- Smoked salmon available in 8 ounce packages in most grocery stores is used with tomatoes and heavy cream for an extravagant and easy to prepare dish.

Preparation Time: 30 minutes

Ingredients:

- 1 pound of Linguine
- 1 four (4) ounce package of smoked salmon, cubed
- 1/4 stick of butter
- 2 tablespoons of olive oil
- 1/2 of a small sweet onion, minced
- 2 whole garlic cloves, minced
- 1/4 pound of *prosciutto*, chopped
- 1 (28) ounce or 1 pound 12 ounce can of whole Italian plum tomatoes, drained and diced
- 1 pint of heavy cream
- 1/2 cup of fresh Italian flat-leaf parsley, chopped
- 1 cup of dry white wine or water
- salt and white pepper to taste

Start the water in a 10-quart saucepan over high heat. Cook the pasta the last 10 minutes of the total preparation time. Warm the butter and olive oil in a saucepan over medium high heat. Add the minced onion and garlic and *soffriggere* or lightly fry for a few minutes. Add the chopped *prosciutto* and simmer for a few minutes. Add the white wine, tomatoes and parsley and continue to simmer for 10 minutes. Add the salmon that you have chopped up into small cubes. Stir the ingredients and simmer for a few minutes. Finally add a pint of heavy cream and simmer all ingredients together for an additional 5 minutes or until the sauce is hot and bubbly. Combine the drained *al dente* linguine with the saucepan ingredients. Toss and mix well. Transfer the completed dish to a large serving bowl. Top with parsley sprigs for garnish. Grind fresh pepper on top and salt to taste. Do not serve with cheese!

Linguine con gli Zucchini e Gamberi- Green summer squash or zucchini with chopped tomatoes and shrimp.

Preparation Time: 30 minutes

Ingredients:

- 1 pound of Linguine
- 1/2 pound or 4 medium sized zucchini, sliced
- 1 pound of large shrimp, shelled and de-veined
- 1 (28) ounce or 1 pound 12 ounce can of whole Italian plum tomatoes, diced
- 6 tablespoons of olive oil
- 1/2 cup of fresh Italian flat-leaf parsley, chopped
- 4 whole garlic cloves, minced
- 1/2 cup of dry white wine
- 2 tablespoons of clam juice
- 1 Knorr®'s chicken bouillon cube

Start the water in a 10-quart saucepan over high heat. Cook the pasta the last 10 minutes of total preparation time. Wash and scrub the zucchini and trim off the stem end. Slice the zucchini into 1/5-inch disks. Meanwhile pre-heat a saucepan over medium high heat adding 4 tablespoons of the olive oil when hot. Add the garlic and *soffriggere* or lightly fry for a few minutes. Add the sliced zucchini sautéing until the zucchini are still crisp and slightly browned. Add the shrimp sautéing until firm and white (about 2-3 minutes). Remove the zucchini and shrimp mixture from the saucepan with a slotted spoon and set aside. Add the white wine, olive oil, tomatoes, parsley, clam juice and crushed bouillon cube to the saucepan and simmer for 10 minutes. Re-add the zucchini/shrimp mixture and cook an additional 3 minutes. Combine the drained *al dente* pasta with the saucepan ingredients. Toss and mix well. Transfer the completed dish to a large serving bowl or platter. Top with a little parsley for garnish.

variation: make it *"arrabbiata"* by adding a pinch of hot pepper flakes.

Spaghetti con Tonno- A quick and delicious tuna pasta dish prepared often by Signora Pelusi, our landlady in Vicenza. Always use the canned, high quality white Albacore tuna in water or oil. Freshly ground black pepper really makes this dish stand out.

Preparation Time: 30 minutes

Ingredients:

- 1 pound of Spaghetti or any other pasta shape
- 1 can of white, Albacore tuna, drained
- 4 tablespoons of olive oil
- 1/2 cup of fresh Italian flat-leaf parsley, chopped
- 1 cup of cooked peas (optional)
- 4 whole garlic cloves, minced
- salt and pepper to taste

Start the water in a 10-quart saucepan over high heat. Cook the pasta until *al dente*. If using frozen peas, you can cook them with the pasta. Add the tuna, minced garlic, peas, parsley and olive oil to the drained *al dente* pasta of any type and toss thoroughly. Add ground pepper and salt to taste. Transfer the completed dish to a large serving bowl. Top with a little parsley for garnish.

variation: make it *"arrabbiata"* by adding a pinch of hot pepper flakes.

Danilo, a fisherman from the seaport of Bari.

114

Chonchiglia con Tonno- A more elaborate preparation of the tuna pasta dish but just as easily thrown together. Always use the canned, high quality white Albacore tuna in water or oil. Fresh ground black pepper really makes this dish stand out.

Preparation Time: 30 minutes

Ingredients:

- 1 pound of small shell pasta or any other pasta shape
- 1 can of white, Albacore tuna, drained
- 4 tablespoons of olive oil
- 1/2 cup of fresh Italian flat-leaf parsley, chopped
- 1 cup of cooked peas
- 1/4 pound of cherry tomatoes, halved
- 1/4 pound of soft mozzarella, cubed
- 2 whole garlic cloves, minced
- salt and pepper to taste

Start the water in a 10-quart saucepan over high heat. Cook the pasta until *al dente*. If using frozen peas, you can cook them with the pasta. Add the tuna, minced garlic, peas, parsley, tomatoes, mozzarella cheese and olive oil to the drained *al dente* pasta of any type and toss thoroughly. Add ground pepper and salt to taste. Transfer the dish to a large serving bowl. Top with a little parsley for garnish.

variation: make it *"arrabbiata"* by adding a pinch of hot pepper flakes.

Rotini con Tonno alla Pugliese (corkscrew pasta with Albacore tuna, artichoke hearts and white kidney beans)- Any pasta could be used. This is a dish typical of my region of Apulia or *Puglia* in Italian. The ingredients of artichokes, beans, and tuna are readily available in *Puglia*.

Preparation Time: 30 minutes

Ingredients:

- 1 pound of Rotini or twists
- 1 can of white, Albacore tuna, drained
- 1 (12) ounce can of artichoke hearts in water or oil, drained and chopped
- 1/2 can of *cannellini* (white kidney beans), drained
- 1/4 each: red, yellow, and green pepper, sliced or julienne or substitute with red peppers from a jar
- 4 tablespoons of olive oil
- 1/4 cup of Italian flat-leaf parsley, chopped
- 2 whole garlic cloves, minced
- 1/2 of a small sweet onion, diced
- 1/2 of a Knorr®'s vegetable bouillon cube
- 1/2 of a cup of water
- salt and pepper to taste

Fill a 10-quart saucepan with water over high heat for the pasta. Add the pasta at the last 10 minutes of the preparation process to the boiling water. Prepare the peppers by halving, de-ribbing and de-seeding them. Place the peppers under a broiler skin side up until the skin is charred black. Remove the peppers, run under cold water, peeling off skin. Slice the peppers into strips and place on a plate. Drizzle a few drops of olive oil on the peppers. Chop the artichokes into small pieces. Pre-heat a saucepan with the olive oil and *soffriggere* or lightly fry the garlic and onions for a few minutes. Add the artichokes, peppers, and parsley to the saucepan and sauté for about 3 minutes. Add the beans, tuna, crushed bouillon cube and water to the saucepan and simmer all ingredients for 5 minutes. Combine the drained *al dente* pasta with the saucepan ingredients. Mix well. Transfer the completed dish to a large serving bowl. Top with parsley sprigs as garnish.

variation: make it *"arrabbiata"* with hot pepper flakes.

Linguine con i Gamberi- Simple dish with shrimp "scampi" style or sautéed in white wine.

Preparation Time: 30 minutes

Ingredients:

- 1 pound of Linguine
- 1 pound of large shrimp, shelled and de-veined
- 1 (28) ounce or 1 pound 12 ounce can of whole Italian plum tomatoes, drained and diced
- 4 tablespoons of olive oil
- 1/2 cup of fresh Italian flat-leaf parsley, chopped
- 4 whole garlic cloves, minced
- 1/2 cup of dry white wine or water
- 2 tablespoons of clam juice
- 1/2 of a Knorr®'s chicken bouillon cube
- salt and pepper to taste

Start the water in a 10-quart saucepan over high heat. Cook the pasta the last 10 minutes of total preparation time. Pre-heat a saucepan over medium high heat adding the olive oil when hot. Add the shrimp and minced garlic sautéing until the shrimp are firm and white (about 2-3 minutes). Remove the shrimp with a slotted spoon and set aside on a platter. Add the white wine, tomatoes, parsley, clam juice and crushed bouillon cube to the saucepan and simmer for 10 minutes. Re-add the shrimp to the saucepan and cook an additional 2 minutes. Combine the drained *al dente* pasta with the saucepan ingredients. Toss and mix well. Transfer the completed dish to a large serving bowl. Top with a little parsley for garnish.

variation: make it *"arrabbiata"* by adding a pinch of hot pepper flakes.

Linguine Barese Cozze e Calamari- A delightful combination of mussels and *calamari* (squid) from the seaport of Bari in Apulia.

Preparation Time: 30 minutes

Ingredients:

- 1 pound of Linguine
- 2 pounds of mussels, soaked, cleaned, and "de-bearded"
- 1/2 pound of *calamari* cut into rings (buy it that way or have the seafood dept. clean and slice it)
- 1 (28 ounce) or 1 pound 12 ounce can of whole Italian plum tomatoes, drained and diced
- 4 tablespoons of olive oil
- 1/2 cup of fresh Italian flat-leaf parsley, chopped
- 4 whole garlic cloves, minced
- 1/2 cup of dry white wine
- 2 tablespoons of clam juice

Start the water in a 10-quart saucepan over high heat. Cook the pasta the last 10 minutes of total preparation time. Scrub the mussels thoroughly. Remove the "beard" protruding from the shell by pulling it out or by using a paring knife. Place the mussels in a bowl and rinse the mussels 2-3 times with cold water to remove any sediment. Discard any mussels that remain open after prodding the inside with a knife. Pre-heat a saucepan with the 2 tablespoons of olive oil. *Soffriggere* or lightly fry 1/2 of the garlic for a few minutes. Add the drained mussels and white wine and simmer over medium high heat with a lid until the mussels open. Remove the mussels with a slotted spoon and reserve the liquid in a separate bowl. Discard any unopened cooked mussels. Strain the mussel juice after allowing any sediment to settle to the bottom of the bowl. Pre-heat the saucepan again, add olive oil, and *soffriggere* or lightly fry the garlic for a few minutes. Add the tomatoes, clam juice, and parsley to the saucepan and simmer for 5 minutes. Add the *calamari* and cook for a few minutes until the *calamari* are white and firm. *Calamari* only need a little heat to be cooked; take care to not overcook them. Re-add the mussels and the strained mussel liquid to the tomato/seafood sauce and simmer over low heat. Combine the drained *al dente* pasta with the saucepan ingredients. Toss or mix well. Transfer the completed dish to a large serving bowl. Top with parsley sprigs for garnish. Grind fresh pepper on top for added flavor and salt to taste. Do not serve with cheese!

Capellini ai Granchi Pugliese- Crab in red sauce with Angel Hair pasta Apulian-style is sweet with a touch of *"arabbiata"* or spiciness.

Preparation Time: 30 minutes

Ingredients:

- 1 pound of Angel Hair pasta (cook only 3-4 minutes)
- 1/2 pound of lump crabmeat (usually in plastic containers in the seafood section)
- 1 (28 ounce) or one pound 12 ounce can of whole Italian plum tomatoes, diced
- 4 tablespoons of olive oil
- 1/2 cup of fresh Italian flat-leaf parsley, chopped
- 4 whole garlic cloves, minced
- pinch of hot pepper flakes
- 2 tablespoons of clam juice
- salt and pepper to taste

Start the water in a 10-quart saucepan over heat. Cook the pasta the last 4 minutes of total preparation time. Heat a saucepan over medium high heat adding the olive oil when hot. *Soffriggere* or lightly fry the minced garlic for a few minutes. Add the tomatoes, hot pepper flakes and parsley to the saucepan and simmer for 10 minutes. Add the crabmeat breaking it up with a fork. Blend the crabmeat into the sauce. Add the clam juice to the sauce and stir. Simmer an additional 5 minutes. Meanwhile add the pasta to the boiling water and cook for 4 minutes. Combine the drained *al dente* pasta with the saucepan ingredients. Toss and mix well. Transfer the pasta to a large serving bowl. Top with a little parsley for garnish. Grind fresh pepper on top for added flavor and salt to taste.

Linguine ed Arista- Lobster can be used to impart a wonderful seafood flavor to your tomato-based sauce. *Aragosta* is the commonly misused term for lobster. *Aragosta* is the Mediterranean spiny lobster that is claw-less and not found in the U.S. market.

Preparation Time: 30 minutes

Ingredients:

- 1 pound of Linguine
- 1 large lobster or 2 medium lobsters, steamed at the store or home
- 1 (28) ounce or one pound 12 ounce can of whole Italian plum tomatoes, diced
- 4 tablespoons of olive oil
- 1/2 cup of fresh Italian flat-leaf parsley, chopped
- 4 whole garlic cloves, minced
- 1/2 cup of dry white wine or water
- 1 can of *Gorton's* minced clams with liquid
- 1/2 of a Knorr®'s fish bouillon cube

Start the water in a 10-quart saucepan over high heat. Cook the pasta the last 10 minutes of total preparation time. To prepare the cooked lobster, remove the succulent meat from the claws and tail. Chop the lobster into small chunks. Set aside in a bowl preserving any liquid from the shell. Pre-heat a saucepan over medium high heat adding the olive oil when hot. Add the minced garlic and *soffriggere* or lightly fry for a few minutes. Add the chopped tomatoes, white wine, parsley, and crushed bouillon cube and simmer for 10 minutes. Add the lobster and canned minced clams with liquid to the saucepan and cook an additional 5 minutes. Combine the drained *al dente* pasta with the lobster, clams and tomatoes in the saucepan. Toss and mix well and cook an additional minute. Transfer the completed dish to a large serving bowl. Top with a little parsley for garnish.

variation: make it *"arrabbiata"* by adding a pinch of hot pepper flakes.

Linguine ed Arista in Bianco- Lobster with a wine/ butter sauce is exquisite.

Preparation Time: 30 minutes

Ingredients:

- 1 pound of Linguine
- 1 large lobster or 2 medium-sized lobsters, steamed at the store or home
- 1/2 stick of sweet butter
- 2 tablespoons of olive oil
- 1/4 cup of fresh Italian flat-leaf parsley, chopped
- 4 whole garlic cloves, minced
- 1 cup of dry white wine or water
- 1 Knorr®'s fish or chicken bouillon cube
- salt and pepper to taste

Start the water in a 10-quart saucepan over high heat. Cook the pasta the last 10 minutes of total preparation time. To prepare the cooked lobster, remove the succulent meat from the claws and tail. Chop the lobster into small chunks. Set aside in a bowl preserving any liquid from the shell. Pre-heat a saucepan over medium high heat adding the olive oil when hot. Add the minced garlic and *soffriggere* or lightly fry for a few minutes. Add the white wine and crushed bouillon and de-glaze over high heat stirring for 2 minutes. Add the lobster with any liquid, parsley and butter and lightly simmer an additional 3 minutes. Combine the drained *al dente* pasta with the lobster and butter-wine sauce in the saucepan. Toss and mix well and cook for 2 additional minutes. Transfer the pasta to a large serving bowl. Top with a little parsley for garnish.

variation: make it *"arrabbiata"* by adding a pinch of hot pepper flakes.

Spaghetti di Mare Cistranese- Mixed seafood in a cream sauce *Cisternino* style.

Preparation Time: 30 minutes

Ingredients:

- 1 pound of Linguine
- 1 large lobster or 2 medium lobsters, steamed at the store or home
- 1/4 pound of sea scallops
- 1/4 pound of crabmeat
- 1/2 stick of sweet butter
- 4 tablespoons of olive oil
- 1/2 cup of fresh Italian flat-leaf parsley, chopped
- 4 whole garlic cloves, minced
- 1/2 cup of dry white wine or water
- 2 pints of double heavy cream
- 1 Knorr®'s fish or chicken bouillon cube

Start the water in a 10-quart saucepan over high heat. Cook the pasta the last 10 minutes of total preparation time. To prepare the cooked lobster, remove the succulent meat from the claws and tail. Chop the lobster into small chunks. Set aside in a bowl preserving any liquid from the shell. Meanwhile pre-heat a saucepan pan over medium high heat adding the olive oil and butter when hot. Add the garlic and *soffriggere* or lightly fry for a few minutes. Add the white wine and bouillon and de-glaze over high heat stirring for 2 minutes. Add the lobster, the raw sea scallops and crab meat with any liquid and simmer until the scallops are firm and white (3-4 minutes). Finally add the heavy cream stir and cook until the cream is bubbly hot. If the sauce isn't thick enough, mix 1 tablespoon of cornstarch with ½ a cup of water, stir and add to the sauce. Combine the drained *al dente* pasta with the lobster, scallop and crab in cream sauce. Toss and mix well and continue cooking for an additional 2 minutes. Transfer the completed dish to a large serving bowl. Top with a little parsley for garnish.

variation: substitute shrimp for the lobster by adding raw shelled, cleaned and de-veined shrimp along with the scallops and crab.

Pasta e Pesce al Forno- Tubular pasta with white fish and spinach smothered in a *besciamela* sauce and baked for 20 minutes. Use leftover baked white fish such as Sea Bass, Flounder etc. to make a quick baked pasta dish.

Preparation Time: 40 minutes

Ingredients:

- 1 pound of Ziti, Penne or Mostacioli (tubular pasta)
- 1/2 to 1 pound of boneless baked white fish (flounder, sea bass, rockfish etc.)
- 1 small bag of fresh spinach or 2 small packages of frozen chopped spinach
- 4 tablespoons of olive oil
- 1/4 cup of fresh Italian flat-leaf parsley, chopped
- salt and white pepper to taste
- 2 whole garlic cloves, minced
- 1/2 of an onion, minced

for the ***besciamella*** sauce (see recipe pg 22)
- 1/2 stick sweet butter
- 1/2 cup all purpose flour
- 4 cups or 2 pints of hot milk
- salt and white pepper to taste
- 1 Knorr®'s chicken bouillon cube
- pinch of nutmeg and cinnamon

Fill a 10-quart saucepan with water over heat for the pasta. Cook the pasta until *al dente* as soon as the pasta water comes to a boil. Drain the pasta in a colander and set aside. While the water is coming to a boil for the pasta, heat a saucepan over medium high heat adding the olive oil when hot. Add the minced garlic and onion and *soffriggere* or lightly fry for a few minutes. Take the fresh cleaned spinach and trim the stems. Place the leaves in the saucepan and sauté until the spinach is limp. Drain any liquid from the spinach. Add the spinach with a dab of olive oil to the bottom of a baking dish. Take the cooked fish and mix it with the cooked pasta and layer that mixture on top of the spinach. Take a saucepan and make a *besciamella* sauce (see recipe on pg. 22) to pour over the dish. Sprinkle the top with a little *parmigiano* cheese and bake in a pre-heated 350° oven until the top browns slightly or for 20 minutes. Remove from the oven and serve. Serve with additional *parmigiano* cheese apart. This is the only seafood dish with cheese.

Pasta con i Gamberi e Finocchio- Wild fennel grows throughout Apulia. Fennel has a slightly licorice and tart taste which compliments seafood and especially grilled fish in a delightful manner.

Preparation Time: 30 minutes

Ingredients:

- 1 pound of Linguine
- 1 pound of large shrimp, shelled and de-veined
- 1 fresh bulb of fennel, cut in julienne style or thin strips (don't use the stems or frond)
- 1 (14.5) ounce can of diced plum tomatoes
- 4 tablespoons of olive oil or as needed
- 1/2 of cup fresh Italian flat-leaf parsley, chopped
- 4 whole garlic cloves, minced
- 1/2 cup of dry white wine or water
- 2 tablespoons of clam juice
- 1 Knorr®'s fish or chicken bouillon cube

Start the water in a 10-quart saucepan over high heat. Cook the pasta the last 10 minutes of total preparation time. Meanwhile heat a saucepan over medium high heat adding the olive oil when hot. Add the fennel, *soffriggere* or lightly fry the fennel until it becomes supple. Add the shrimp and garlic sautéing until the shrimp take color and are firm. Do not overcook. Remove the shrimp with a slotted spoon and place them on a plate. Add the white wine, tomatoes, parsley, clam juice and crushed bouillon cube to the saucepan. Simmer for 10 minutes over medium high heat. Re-add the shrimp and cook an additional 2 minutes. Combine the drained *al dente* pasta with the shrimp, fennel and tomatoes in the saucepan. Toss/mix well and continue cooking for an additional 2 minutes. Transfer the completed dish to a large serving bowl. Top with a little parsley and olive oil for garnish.

variation: make it *"arrabbiata"* by adding a pinch of hot pepper flakes.

Spaghetti con le Cozze e Gamberi (Mussels and Shrimp)- This dish combines mussels and shrimp. Try to find the large scampi if you can but if unsuccessful use jumbo shrimp.

Preparation Time: 30 minutes

Ingredients:

- 1 pound of Spaghetti
- 1 pound of fresh mussels (*cozze*)
- 10 Jumbo shrimp (shelled and de-veined)
- 6 tablespoons of olive oil or as needed
- 2 zucchini, julienne or cut in thin slices
- 1 (14.5) ounce can of diced tomatoes
- 1/2 cup of fresh Italian flat-leaf parsley, chopped
- 4 whole garlic cloves, minced
- 1 cup of dry white wine or water
- salt and pepper to taste

Start the water in a 10-quart saucepan over high heat. Cook the pasta the last 10 minutes of total preparation time. Scrub the mussels thoroughly. Remove the "beard" protruding from the shell by pulling it out or by using a paring knife. Place the mussels in a bowl and rinse the mussels 2-3 times with cold water to remove any sediment. Discard any mussels that remain open after prodding the inside with a knife. Pre-heat a saucepan with 4 tablespoons of olive oil. Add half of the garlic, and sauté in olive oil until the garlic takes on a little color. Add the drained mussels, parsley and white wine and sauté with a lid over the saucepan for 5 minutes or until the mussels open. Remove the mussels with a slotted spoon and reserve the liquid in a separate bowl. Discard any unopened cooked mussels. Strain the mussel juice after allowing any sediment to settle to the bottom of the bowl. Meanwhile add the pasta to the water. Pre-heat a saucepan with olive oil over medium high heat. *Soffriggere* or lightly fry the garlic, tomatoes, zucchini and parsley for 8 minutes. Add the shrimp and sauté until the shrimp are just firm and white. Re-add the mussels and the strained mussel liquid with the tomatoes, shrimp and zucchini mixture that is in the saucepan and keep warm over low heat. Combine the drained *al dente* pasta with the saucepan ingredients. Toss and mix well and cook an additional 2 minutes. Transfer the completed dish to a large serving bowl. Top with parsley sprigs for garnish.

Linguine con le Vongole e Pancetta- This dish adds the smoky flavor of ham to the Linguine along with tomatoes and leeks.

Preparation Time: 30 minutes

Ingredients:

- 1 pound of Linguine
- 2 cans of *Gorton's®* minced or chopped clams with liquid
- 10 cherry tomatoes, halved
- 6 tablespoons of olive oil
- 4 ounces of *pancetta* or bacon, chopped
- 1/2 cup of fresh Italian flat-leaf parsley, chopped
- 1/4 cup of pitted, chopped green *Cerignola* olives or substitute chopped stuffed olives with pimiento
- 2 cups of leeks, chopped
- 4 whole garlic cloves, minced
- 1/2 cup of dry white wine or water
- 1 Knorr®'s chicken bouillon cube
- salt and pepper to taste

Start the water in a 10-quart saucepan over high heat. Cook the pasta the last 10 minutes of total preparation time. Pre-heat a saucepan with the 4 tablespoons of olive oil. Add the garlic, *pancetta,* tomatoes and leeks and *soffriggere* or lightly fry for a few minutes until the *pancetta* is firm. Add the white wine or water, bouillon and olives and simmer over medium heat for 5 minutes. Add the canned minced clams with liquid, and parsley and cook over low heat for 5 minutes. Combine the drained *al dente* pasta with the clam sauce in the saucepan. Toss, mix well and cook an additional 2 minutes. Transfer the completed dish to a large serving bowl. Top with parsley sprigs for garnish. Grind fresh pepper on top for added flavor and salt to taste. *Per carita',* please do not serve this dish with cheese!

Spaghetti col Filetto di Pesce- Tilapia or other white fish fillet with tomatoes and pine nuts.

Preparation Time: 20 minutes

Ingredients:

- 1 pound of Spaghetti
- 4 white fish fillets
- 6 canned whole plum tomatoes, diced
- 2 tablespoons of pine nuts
- 1/2 cup of fresh Italian flat-leaf parsley, chopped
- 2 whole garlic cloves, minced
- 1/2 cup of dry white wine or water
- 1/2 Knorr®'s chicken or fish bouillon cube
- 6 tablespoons or so of olive oil (qb –quanto basta in Italian)
- salt and pepper to taste

Start the water in a 10-quart saucepan over high heat. Cook the pasta the last 10 minutes of total preparation time. Pre-heat a saucepan with the 6 tablespoons of olive oil. Add the garlic, pine nuts, a little parsley and tomatoes and *soffriggere* or lightly fry for a few minutes. Add the white fish fillets cooking on both sides for a few minutes. Add the white wine or water and bouillon and simmer over medium heat for 5 minutes. Combine the drained *al dente* pasta with the fish and sauce in the saucepan. Toss and mix carefully. Transfer the completed dish to a large serving bowl. Top with parsley sprigs for garnish. Grind fresh pepper on top for added flavor and salt to taste.

LA FAMIGLIA PENTASSUGLIA. My Aunts and Uncles along with my Mom, Christina.

Melanzane al Forno- Special Eggplant Lasagna recipe- Not a typical recipe for this cookbook. I included this recipe upon request from some friends. This recipe combines the non-ribbed flat lasagna noodles with fried eggplant, meat sauce and besciamella sauce.

Preparation Time: 60 minutes

Ingredients:

For the red sauce:
- Olive oil, (qb) or as needed
- 4 cloves of garlic minced
- 1 small onion ,or half of a large sweet onion, minced
- Fresh Italian parsley, diced
- 2 stalks of celery, minced
- ¼ lb each or ground beef, turkey or veal or pork
- 2 TBS of tomato paste
- One, 1 lb 12 ounce can of crushed tomatoes
- Oregano or basil, dried

:
Soffriggere or lightly fry the celery, parsley or basil, onion and garlic for a few minutes. Sauté the ground meat until browned. Add the tomato paste, stir then add crushed tomatoes, herbs to taste. Simmer for 20 minutes.

For the eggplant:
- Lots of vegetable oil
- Eggs, beaten
- 2 cups of flour for eggplant
- large bag of shredded mozzarella cheese
- Grated *parmigiano* cheese, a few cups for topping the eggplant
- 3 large eggplants, sliced lengthwise
- 2 small boxes of flat no-boil lasagna noodles
- Sliced cooked deli-ham or *prosciutto cotto*

In a hot pan, heat the oil. Slice eggplant lengthwise about 1/4 inch thick. Remove outside peel if desired. Dip in egg wash and then flour. Fry the eggplant until light golden brown and sprinkle *parmigiano* cheese on top. Set aside

For the Besciamella: or see recipe on page 22
- 3 pints of heavy cream or full milk
- ½ stick of butter
- 3 TBS of flour or as needed
- ½ Knorr's chicken bouillon cube
- Corn starch dissolved in water as an extra thickener if needed

On low heat melt butter, add flour and make a roux or paste, turn up heat to medium high and slowly add warm milk, stir with whisk continuously until thick if not thick enough for add a little corn starch dissolved in water. Add the 1/2 of the bouillon cube and whisk until dissolved. Set aside.

Assemble the dish in a rectangular baking or lasagna pan in the following order:
- One layer eggplant
- Meat sauce on the eggplant
- Slice of thinly sliced cooked ham
- Mozzarella cheese
- Lasagna noodles
- Sprinkle grated *parmigiano* cheese on each layer
- Repeat ingredients in layers
- Top with the besciamella
- Cook at 350° for 40 minutes with foil covering the dish..
- Take foil off and brown the last few minutes.

Have a little red sauce on the side to use as a topping if desired.

Alberobello, City of Trulli

Alberobello is an entire town of *Trulli* houses. Normally *Trulli* houses are only found in the countryside of the Valley of Itria in Apulia. In 1480 the Aragonese Spanish rulers in Naples commanded Giulio Antonio I of Acquaviva to put together an Army to repel the invading Ottoman Turks at Otranto. He did so and was awarded the zone that is today Alberobello for himself and his successors, the Counts of Conversano. Since new construction in the zone had to be approved from Naples by royal edits, the Count of Conversano cleverly found a method to avoid paying new taxes. To avoid royal taxes on new construction, the Count of Conversano mandated that all new construction be *Trulli* houses that are built of unmortared stone. In this manner, he could quickly order the *Trulli* to be taken down as if they had never been constructed.

Grandparents or Nonni in their younger years

Trullo near Fasano

Grandad's Trullo today

Trullo Church in Alberobello

132